MANAGING BORDERS IN AN INCREASINGLY BORDERLESS WORLD

Randall Hansen and Demetrios G. Papademetriou, Editors

December 2013

© 2013 Migration Policy Institute
All Rights Reserved.

No part of this publication may be reproduced or transmitted in any form by any means, electronic or mechanical, including photocopy, or any information storage and retrieval system, without permission from the Migration Policy Institute. Permission for reproducing excerpts from this volume can be found at www.migrationpolicy.org/about/copy.php. Inquiries can also be directed to: Permissions Department, Migration Policy Institute, 1400 16th Street, NW, Suite 300, Washington, DC 20036, or by contacting communications@migrationpolicy.org.

Library of Congress Cataloging-in-Publication Data

Managing borders in an increasingly borderless world / edited by Randall Hansen and Demetrios G. Papademetriou.

pages cm

Includes bibliographical references.

ISBN 978-0-9831591-2-4

1. Border Security. 2. Boundaries. 3. Globalization. 4. Emigration and Immigration--Government policy. I. Hansen, Randall. II. Papademetriou, Demetrios G.

HV6181.M36 2013

325--dc23

2013022842

Library and Archives Canada Cataloguing in Publication

Managing borders in an increasingly borderless world / Randall Hansen and Demetrios G. Papademetriou, editors.

Includes bibliographical references.
ISBN 978-0-9831591-2-4 (pbk.)

1. Border security--Case studies. I. Hansen, Randall, author, editor of compilation II. Papademetriou, Demetrios G., author, editor of compilation III. Migration Policy Institute, issuing body
JV6225.M35 2013   320.1'2   C2013-905305-0

Cover Photo: Modified version of "World Map" by Comstock images, via Photos.com, Image ID 78492474.
Cover Design: April Siruno, MPI
Typesetting: Erin Perkins, LeafDev

Suggested citation: Hansen, Randall and Demetrios G. Papademetriou, eds. 2013. *Managing Borders in an Increasingly Borderless World*. Washington, DC: Migration Policy Institute.

Printed in the United States of America.

TABLE OF CONTENTS

FOREWORD 1
    Randall Hansen and Demetrios G. Papademetriou

**CHAPTER 1: Securing Borders: The Intended, Unintended, and Perverse
    Consequences** 3
    Randall Hansen and Demetrios G. Papademetriou

**CHAPTER 2: Challenges to the Common European Asylum System:
    The Dublin Rules Under Judicial Pressure** 23
    Kay Hailbronner

CHAPTER 3: Border Insecurity in Central America's Northern Triangle 45
    Ralph Espach and Daniel Haering

**CHAPTER 4: Human Smuggling and Trafficking into Europe:
    A Comparative Perspective** 69
    Louise Shelley

CHAPTER 5: North America's Borders: Finding the Future 95
    Brian Grant and Christopher Sands

**CHAPTER 6: Faltering Schengen Cooperation?
    The Challenges to Maintaining a Stable System** 107
    Elizabeth Collett

ACKNOWLEDGMENTS 133

ABOUT THE EDITORS AND AUTHORS 135

ABOUT THE MIGRATION POLICY INSTITUTE 139

**ABOUT THE MUNK SCHOOL OF GLOBAL AFFAIRS,
    UNIVERSITY OF TORONTO** 140

FOREWORD

As this volume goes to print, the United States is closer to passing large-scale immigration reform than at any time in the past three decades, with border control at the very heart of this debate. Indeed, the success of comprehensive immigration reform is entirely contingent upon guaranteeing, or at least convincing a still-anxious public, that there is a secure southern border — even if there is no agreement on what "success" in this regard might look like. This volume showcases approaches toward border management in Europe, Central America, and North America, and reflects on the challenges that countries in these regions face in managing their borders.

In an ideal world, secure borders would ensure that the movements we want — such as legal goods, tourists, students, and business people — can flow unimpeded across borders, while unwanted movements — such as terrorists, drugs, weapons, and unauthorized migrants — are blocked. Given that there is no single policy tool that alone can achieve this result, governments must deploy an elusive combination of policies and programs, depending on the context.

Countries face an array of challenges to securing their borders, complicated by the underlying paradox that fortified borders inherently attract smugglers. As long as there is demand to cross, there will be people who profit by evading border controls and facilitating this movement.

In today's climate of increasing globalization and technological innovation, borders are not just physical barriers through which goods and people cross, but virtual sites of cash transfers, trade flows, and international business connections. As such, border security policy is expanding to include sophisticated intelligence gathering and analysis to intercept illicit transactions before they reach the border. Additionally, innovations like the United States' Global Entry program allow expedited clearance for pre-approved, low-risk travelers — highlighting how border security efforts are increasingly located beyond the physical border between countries.

In Europe, the central challenge lies in the need for European Union countries to balance their national interests with those of greater regional cooperation. However, northern and southern Member States often take differing views on what constitutes equitable burden-sharing.

Attempts to manage borders in Central America's Northern Triangle (Guatemala, Honduras, and El Salvador) are complicated by widespread corruption, weak institutions, and a coordination gap between relevant agencies and national and local governments across and within countries.

In North America, Canada, Mexico, and the United States have struggled to fortify the border post-9/11, including instituting new technology, which has brought with it an amalgam of challenges and controversies.

This edited volume brings together perspectives from both sides of the Atlantic on what border security means in practice, the solutions that continue to evade policymakers, and what policies have been the most (and least) successful in the pursuit of "secure" borders. While border management contexts vary throughout the world, they share at least one commonality: at the core, strong states and institutions are fundamental to secure borders.

Randall Hansen
University of Toronto

Demetrios G. Papademetriou
Migration Policy Institute

CHAPTER I

SECURING BORDERS: THE INTENDED, UNINTENDED, AND PERVERSE CONSEQUENCES

Randall Hansen
University of Toronto

Demetrios G. Papademetriou
Migration Policy Institute

I. Introduction

This chapter outlines the security-related challenges that borders are intended to address and, in turn, the perverse consequences (both predictable and not) that tighter border enforcement generates. It approaches the topic of borders and security thematically, outlining the major security issues faced by most states. Country-specific examples are used to illustrate these difficulties. It then considers the consequences of efforts to control borders. These challenges are grouped under five categories: terrorism, asylum, human smuggling and trafficking, illegal migration, and drug trafficking.

The chapter proceeds in three steps. First, it begins with definitional and conceptual issues, defining borders and security and reflecting on the character of borders as a policy area. Second, it reviews the major challenges that states face in securing borders. Finally, it outlines policy recommendations for discussion purposes.

II. Defining Borders and Security

There is a basic — and constantly evolving[1] — relationship between borders and security. *Borders* delineate the boundaries of sovereign states. As no state is hermetically sealed, and all are effectively open for legitimate trade and transactions such as money transfers, borders are porous — though to what degree varies greatly. For example, the United Kingdom's borders in the late Victorian period were as porous as possible, since there was effectively no control on the movement of people or goods. In a contemporary context, most borders within Central America and Central Asia are virtually unpatrolled. The borders of the Soviet Union, which allowed a trickle of temporary and almost no permanent movement, were as restricted as possible (as are North Korea's borders today). And there are many points in between.

All border policies aim for two sets of related goals. First, they want to ensure that movement deemed beneficial (e.g., of legal goods, most tourists, some categories of students, business people, and certain categories of migrants) is unimpeded; while unwanted movement (of drugs, other unauthorized goods, and unauthorized migrants) is blocked. The costs of failed border policy can be enormous. After the September 11, 2001 attacks, the United States responded by grounding all flights and essentially closing its borders. Within hours, there was a 50-mile backup at the Windsor-Detroit Bridge, through which most vehicle-based trade between Canada and the United States passes. Border delays today — which in large part continue to stem from the stringency of post-9/11 border security measures — added about $800 to the price of every new vehicle manufactured in North America.[2]

Second, states want to give the impression that all people within their borders — whether citizens, legal residents, or unauthorized migrants — are receiving fair and equal treatment. When unwanted migrants are disproportionately associated with particular ethnic or national groups, this task is particularly challenging. Many activists in Europe and North America believe that border controls are inherently biased by race and class considerations, citing the disproportionate targeting of nationals of certain states and of nonwhite migrants.

Both democratic states (those with free elections, alternating governments, and independent judiciaries) and non-democratic ones face

---

1 Collecting customs and duties, a traditional function of border posts, is certainly on the decline; trade agreements have eliminated many such revenues, and today most duties do not necessarily have to be collected at borders. At the same time, illegitimate financial transactions — often associated with terrorism and, in some corridors, the profits from drugs and other illegal transactions — are the new frontier of border control.

2 Laura Dawson, "The Canada-U.S. Border Action Plan: This Time It's For Real, Charlie Brown," in *A Safe and Smart Border: The Ongoing Quest in U.S.-Canada Relations* (One Issue Two Voices series, issue 15, The Wilson Center, September 2012): 9, www.wilsoncenter.org/sites/default/files/CI_120828_One%20Issue%20Two%20Voices%2015_FINAL.pdf.

identical challenges. They only differ in the range of options they have in responding to them. Non-democratic states such as China and most Middle Eastern and Gulf states pursue the same goals as democratic states, with two important differences: they often do not recognize a right of exit, and they are less concerned about appearing fair and just in their treatment of different classes of migrants.

Security is understood for the purposes of this chapter in negative terms: an absence of unwanted movement across borders.[3] Fully secure borders are free of terrorists, unauthorized and other unwanted migrants, the smuggling of drugs and contraband goods, and smuggled and trafficked people. Of course, borders are never perfectly secure; achieving security is thus invariably a matter of relative success.

III. Challenges to Border Security

A. Shifting Borders

Border policy has seen great transformations in recent decades due to the evolution of border security. Most dramatically, the European Union (EU) removed internal border controls for the members of the Schengen zone.[4] Other countries, too, have changed their ways. The United States has had preclearance facilities in some Canadian airports for decades (and has expanded them to all major Canadian airports in recent years) and now has such facilities in Ireland (in Shannon and Dublin), the Bahamas, Bermuda, and Aruba. And all major immigrant-receiving states have delegated certain immigration controls to private actors, notably airline and shipping companies.[5] All these measures are designed to push the border outward, to create distance between any attempt to reach the legal borders of a state and the act of reaching the soil of the country itself.

As borders have expanded outwards, they have also expanded inwards. The often-ignored corollary of the Schengen Agreement was the expansion of internal checks and a mutually recognized right to

---

3   The focus on security here is restricted to national, or state, security. "Human security," a currently booming field of social science inquiry, covers the economic and social conditions of particular human populations, and is outside the scope of this chapter.
4   The Schengen Agreement, signed in 1985, theoretically creates a "borderless" zone among the parties to the agreement. Once inside the zone, a person is able to travel to any member country without needing a passport.
5   Gallya Lahav and Virginie Guiraudon, "Comparative Perspectives on Border Control: Away from the Border and Outside the State," in *The Wall around the West: State Borders and Immigration Controls in North America and Europe*, eds. Peter Andreas and Timothy Snyder (Lanham, MD: Rowman and Littlefield, 2000); Otwin Marenin,"Democratic Oversight and Border Management: Principles, Complexity, and Agency Interests," in *Borders and Security Governance*, eds. Marina Caparini and Otwin Marenin (Geneva: Geneva Centre for the Democratic Control of Armed Forces, 2006).

pursue criminals across borders. The latter resulted in much higher levels of cooperation across states in targeting criminal activity. On one level, this move is highly consistent with the continental model of border control, which combines checks at the borders with checks *within* borders (hence the requirement to carry identity cards on the European continent, which Europeans regard as anodyne, and which North Americans would consider an offensive and unwarranted invasion of privacy).

In the North American context, by contrast, the border evolved over the course of the 20th century as more of a firewall: you cross it with great difficulty, but once you cross, you are left alone. This approach has been changing in recent years, however, as several US states (such as Alabama, Arizona, Georgia, Indiana, South Carolina, and Utah) have passed laws requiring that police officers and other state officials check the immigration status of suspected unauthorized migrants. These laws are highly controversial; they raise jurisdictional issues and the federal government has challenged them. In July 2012, the US Supreme Court delivered a decision in *United States v. Arizona*, a case that the Obama administration brought against Arizona's 2010 immigration law. In a split decision, the high court struck down three provisions: (1) the requirement that immigrants carry registration documents or face misdemeanor charges; (2) the transformation of job-seeking by unauthorized migrants into a criminal offense; and (3) the obligation that police officers stop without a warrant anyone they suspect of having violated US immigration law.[6] It did, however, uphold one provision, which requires state and local police in Arizona to check the immigration status of anyone they stop or arrest if they suspect the person has entered or remained in the country illegally. Both the original law and the portion that survived the Supreme Court decision reflect a greater American interest in controlling the border after migrants pass through it. The physical border itself and the border guards who screen, detect, detain, and prevent unauthorized migrants, still clearly matter.[7] But they are nested in a much wider range of internal and external policies designed to protect the border.

B. Governing Borders

In most countries, the border is controlled by a specific agency: US Customs and Border Protection, the Canada Border Services Agency, the French Direction central de la police aux frontières, or the German Bundespolizei. Such agencies are generally answerable to interior

---

[6] Robert Barnes, "Supreme Court upholds key part of Arizona law for now, strikes down other provisions," *Washington Post*, June 25, 2012, http://articles.washingtonpost.com/2012-06-25/politics/35461864_1_immigration-decision-arizona-law-illegal-immigrants; John Schwartz, "Supreme Court Decision on Arizona Immigration Law," *New York Times*, June 26, 2012, www.nytimes.com/interactive/2012/06/26/us/scotus-immigrationlaw-analysis.html?_r=0.

[7] Marenin, "Democratic Oversight and Border Management."

ministries or their equivalents. Like immigration policy more generally, the implementation of border policy cuts across ministries: interior, justice, and foreign affairs all have a role in the area. (There is often tension between interior and foreign affairs ministries; the former view visas as a basic policy instrument, the latter as a major international irritant).[8] Finally, the military plays a complementary role in border control. National air forces deal with violations of air space; in the United States the US Coast Guard falls under the jurisdiction of the US Department of Homeland Security (DHS).[9]

C. Embedded Borders

Border policy relies on actions and developments beyond the control of any nation-state. This is of course true in other areas, such as economic policy: changes in global economic conditions can suddenly derail national economic plans. But even in this area, states possess instruments in fiscal and monetary policy that allow them to shape the national and — depending on the size of the country — international economy. Border policy, by contrast, is reactive. It must respond to the changing nature and flows of international threats and migrants (which are themselves affected by the international economy), including sudden influxes and the latest moves by migrant traffickers. The state can naturally do all that is possible to make its own border impervious to clandestine crossings, but at best, it has an indirect and uncertain effect on the domestic conditions of other states — notably unemployment, limited economic opportunities, and in extreme cases, war — that encourage emigration.

D. Terrorism

The most commonly cited threat to border security is terrorism. Here the picture is particularly complex. The problem is partly definitional: the term *terrorism* means so many different things to different people (one person's terrorist being another's freedom fighter) that some scholars have concluded that it cannot be defined.[10] Even if one accepts that terrorism is recognizable to its victims, if not definable, placing it is nearly impossible. Terrorists often come from within the country

---

8   On this topic in the context of the Schengen negotiations, see Virginie Guiraudon, "Enlisting Third Parties in Border Control: A Comparative Study of its Causes and Consequences," in *Borders and Security Governance*, eds. Marina Caparini and Otwin Marenin (Geneva: Geneva Centre for the Democratic Control of Armed Forces, 2006).

9   The US Coast Guard answers to the Department of Homeland Security (DHS) during peacetime, but the executive can transfer responsibility to the US Navy in the event of war. At times, the US National Guard is enlisted in border-control activities. Moreover, DHS has developed its own air arm, which is growing apace. During the Cold War, the German border-control police enjoyed combat status so that they could be immediately switched to a frontline army in the event that the Soviets acted on plans for a conventional attack on Western Europe.

10 Walter Laqueur, *The Age of Terrorism* (London: Little Brown, 1988).

themselves: the Irish Republican Army in Northern Ireland, the Red Army Faction in West Germany, and more recently, the 7/7 bombers in London, were all indigenous terrorists. Yet in other cases — the 9/11 bombers; the shoe bomber, Richard Reid; the terrorists involved in a 2006 transatlantic aircraft plot using liquid explosives; and the millennium bomber, Ahmed Ressam — the crossing of borders was essential to the crime. Alhough these failed or successful attacks all involved airports, terrorists may also move through land borders and ports (but strikingly few cases of such movement have been publicly identified). Airports, ports, and land borders are frequent targets of attack — or they may be the entry points through which terrorists pass.[11]

E. Illegal Migration

Illegal migration competes with terrorism for the most visible threat to borders, and with good reason: illegal migration is a direct repudiation of the border itself. As a category, illegal migration encompasses many types of security threats: terrorists, criminals, smugglers, traffickers, and so on. For the overwhelming majority of migrants, however, irregular migration is not followed by illegal, let alone violent, behavior: the vast majority of unauthorized migrants lead peaceful lives — residing, studying, working, and often paying taxes in the country they entered illegally.

Unauthorized migrants evade the border in two major ways. The first is by overstaying — that is, by crossing borders legally as tourists or students and then staying past the date by which they were to return. Estimates of overstayers in the United States range from 25 to 40 percent of the unauthorized population[12] (and the proportion is much higher in the European Union). The second is illegally crossing the border itself and then staying.

Data on the total number of unauthorized migrants are not fully reliable, but the Migration Policy Institute (MPI) estimates the number of illegal migrants in Europe to be between 1.9 and 3.8 million in 2011.[13] In the United States, DHS estimated the unauthorized population at

---

11   K. Jack Riley, "Border Control," in *The McGraw-Hill Homeland Security Handbook*, ed. David Kamien (Santa Monica, CA: Rand Publication): 595; Lahav and Guiraudon, "Comparative Perspectives on Border Control: Away from the Border and Outside the State."
12   Jeffrey Passel, *Unauthorized Migrants: Numbers and Characteristics* (Washington, DC: Pew Research Center, 2005), http://pewhispanic.org/files/reports/46.pdf.
13   Christal Morehouse and Michael Blomfield, *Irregular Migration in Europe* (Washington, DC: Migration Policy Institute, 2011), www.migrationpolicy.org/pubs/tcmirregularmigration.pdf. On regularization as response to these movements, see Kate Brick, *Regularizations in the European Union: The Contentious Policy Tool* (Washington, DC: Migration Policy Institute, 2011), www.migrationpolicy.org/pubs/EURegularization-Insight.pdf.

11.5 million in January 2011,[14] a figure that is very close to the estimate of independent researchers.

F. Asylum Seekers

Asylum seekers present particular challenges to border management, because it is in the area of asylum that international law most severely restricts state sovereignty. When asylum seekers declare themselves at the borders of states that have signed the United Nations' 1951 *Convention relating to the Status of Refugees* and/or its 1967 amending protocol, these states are under an obligation not to return asylum seekers to countries in which their lives could be threatened. In addition, since the signing of the convention, most states or their courts have articulated complex and lengthy legal procedures for processing and appeal, which make full asylum processing both time-consuming and expensive. When asylum seekers are legitimate refugees, there is little the states can or should want to do about it. This is, however, typically not the case. Recognition rates (that is, the proportion of asylum seekers granted refugee status under the 1951 Convention) in Europe rarely exceed 10 percent. Even when including nonconvention statuses, they usually hover around 30 percent and never top 50 percent.[15] In all states, therefore, asylum streams contain large numbers of people who are *not* convention refugees, and who in most cases are economic migrants. The fact that many of those ineligible for protection cannot be returned — because they come from failed states, states that might not be able to protect them effectively, or states that have refused to sign readmission agreements with receiving countries — makes asylum one of the most difficult and divisive "border policy" issues.

G. Smuggling and Trafficking

Illegal migration is in many ways inseparable from smuggling and trafficking. Both involve the illegal movement of people, but the difference between them is in the relationship between transporters and migrants. In the case of smuggling, the relationship is consensual and ends once the migrants have passed border controls, and once other elements of the transaction (such as financial arrangements or delivery

---

14　Michael Hoefer, Nancy Rytina, and Bryan Baker, *Estimates of the Unauthorized Immigrant Population Residing in the United States: January 2011* (Washington, DC: Department of Homeland Security Office of Immigration Statistics, 2012), www.dhs.gov/sites/default/files/publications/ois_ill_pe_2011.pdf.

15　See Eric Neumayer, "Asylum Recognition Rates in Western Europe: Their Determinants, Variation, and Lack of Convergence," *Journal of Conflict Resolution* 49, no. 1 (2005): 43–66.

to a specific destination) have been completed.[16] On the other hand, the trafficked migrant is forcefully transited against his or her will, or remains in a relationship of dependence — through work, payment, or the coerced provision of sexual or other services — after having passed immigration controls.

According to the United Nations Office on Drugs and Crime (UNODC) research on smuggling, the global patterns of smuggling include:[17]

- *Involvement of organized criminals.* Criminals are controlling an increasing proportion of the "trade" in smuggled migrants. Criminal organizations are increasingly providing smuggling services to unauthorized migrants. As a result, the majority of unauthorized migrants now rely on smugglers or traffickers.

- *High risks and high profits.* Demand, associated risks, and barriers to entry into the "business" are all extremely high. These factors, in turn, keep profits high, making smuggling increasingly attractive to the most sophisticated criminals — ones with large, international professional networks.

- *Varied smuggling methods.* Smugglers use very different methods, and so the experience of being smuggled varies immensely. Some use highly sophisticated and expensive services such as forged documents and fraudulent visas, while others use low-cost methods such as illegal transport in trucks, small boats, or containers. In some cases, smuggling can resemble genteel, white-collar crime; in others — such as smugglers who rape, rob, beat, and leave to die Central American and Mexican migrants trying to get in the United States — it resembles torture. Generally speaking, the cheaper the method, the greater the risk to the migrant. Deaths due to drowning or suffocation in trucks and containers, or dehydration in the desert, are common.

- *Deadly conditions.* There are probably thousands of deaths due to smuggling each year. For many of those who arrive alive, the conditions en route are appalling.

It is notoriously difficult to obtain reliable information on smuggling and trafficking. A small study (involving 169 cases) of smuggled

---

16   Formally, smuggling is defined as "the procurement, in order to obtain, directly or indirectly, a financial or material benefit, of the illegal entry of a person into a State Party of which the person is not a national or a permanent resident." See United Nations General Assembly, *Protocol against the Smuggling of Migrants by Land, Sea, and Air, Supplementing the United Nations Convention against Transnational Organized Crime*, November 15, 2000, Article 3, www.refworld.org/docid/479dee062.html.

17   United Nations Office on Drugs and Crime (UNODC), *Smuggling of Migrants* (Vienna: UNODC, 2009), www.unodc.org/documents/human-trafficking/Migrant_Smuggling/09-81206_English_eBook.pdf.

migrants from Tamil Nadu in southern India identified a number of patterns that might also apply in other cases:[18]

- Destinations varied, and encompassed much of the world. Some 25 percent of smuggled migrants planned to travel to Europe (the United Kingdom was particularly popular, but all countries were targets); other destinations included the United States, Canada, Kuwait, Thailand, Malaysia, and Dubai. Some of these countries may have been jumping-off points — a forged Malaysian passport was particularly popular because of the visa-free travel it afforded.

- Unemployment and poverty were the major push factors.

- Smuggled migrants were 89 percent male and disproportionately young (43 percent were under age 30, and 55 percent under age 40).

- Almost all smuggled migrants relied on forged documents. The main techniques smugglers used were false "Emigration Certificate Not Required" stamps for leaving India, photo substitution, and restitched passports.

- The cost of these services was very high: travel to the United Kingdom cost between $12,000 and $15,000. The cheapest destinations were in the Middle East, at $2,000 to $3,000.

While the numbers are inexact, we can say with confidence that the majority — and probably the *vast majority* — of unauthorized migrants are smuggled. The numbers of trafficked migrants are much smaller, but far too high given the nature of the crime. In 2005, the International Labor Organization (ILO) estimated that there are 2.4 million people in forced labor, including sexual exploitation, at any given time.[19] Unlike unauthorized migrants, who are mostly in developed countries, trafficked migrants are represented in significant numbers in the developing world. ILO estimates that there are about 1.36 million trafficked forced laborers in Asia and the Pacific; 230,000 in the Middle East and North Africa; 130,000 in sub-Saharan Africa; 250,000 in Latin America; and 270,000 in the industrialized countries.[20]

---

18   K. C. Saha, *Smuggling of Migrants from India to Europe and in Particular to UK: A Study on Tamil Nadu* (New Delhi: UNODC, 2009), www.unodc.org/documents/human-trafficking/ Smuggling_of_Migrants_from_India.pdf.
19   International Labor Organization (ILO), *A Global Alliance against Forced Labour* (Geneva: International Labor Office, 2005): 10, www.ilo.org/public/english/standards/relm/ilc/ ilc93/pdf/rep-i-b.pdf.
20   Ibid., 14.

H. Drug Trafficking and Other Criminal Activity

The drug-trafficking business is estimated to generate over $300 billion in sales internationally.[21] It is associated with criminal activities on the part of traffickers and dealers (including organized-crime groups), and the perhaps unwitting participation of consumers, who fund crime through consumption. As drug production is strictly controlled in Europe, North America, Australia, and New Zealand, but demand and resources there are high, drugs that are grown — cocaine and cannabis — are trafficked internationally.[22] Cannabis, for instance, is mostly produced in Morocco, Mexico, Afghanistan, Nepal, and India, but 49 percent of cannabis resin seizures take place in Europe and 70 percent of cannabis seizures occur in North America.[23] The trade is largely interregional: most of the cannabis in Europe originates in Morocco.[24] The vast majority of profits from the drug business go to traffickers, with organized-crime groups taking around 10 percent of the profits.[25] In Mexico and Central America, where organized-crime groups have increasingly taken over the drug-trafficking market, this percentage is much higher.

Border control is one, but only one, element of anti-drug policy. The United States, which has the most developed anti-drug strategy among countries, has based its strategy on three main pillars: domestic education and prevention among users, crop eradication, and interdiction.[26] Only the last of these relates to borders. Some 26 percent of the US federal drug control budget ($12.6 billion in 2007) goes to interdiction.[27] Interdiction involves disrupting the narcotics trade abroad through the training of local officials and elimination of crops, and blocking actual drug traffickers crossing US borders. In anti-drug policy, the border is the last — and often unsuccessful — line of defense, since no border is entirely secure.

Focusing narrowly on these three pillars has clearly not been anywhere near adequate. Former Arizona Attorney General Terry Goddard points out in his three-part series of articles titled *How to Fix a Broken*

---

21 Niklas Pollard, "UN report puts world's illicit drug trade at estimated $321b," Reuters, June 30, 2005.
22 Chemically produced drugs, such as ecstasy-group substances and amphetamines, consumed in Europe are mostly produced in Europe. UNODC, *World Drug Report 2011* (New York: UNODC, 2011): 38, www.unodc.org/documents/data-and-analysis/WDR2011/World_Drug_Report_2011_ebook.pdf.
23 UNODC, *World Drug Report 2011*, 18, 35–36.
24 Ibid., 21.
25 Ibid., 46.
26 Raphael F. Perl, *International Drug Trade and US Foreign Policy* (Washington, DC: Congressional Research Service, 2006): 2-5, https://opencrs.com/document/RL33582/.
27 Ibid.

Border[28] that drug policy needs to incorporate three additional interrelated elements:

1. Hitting the cartels that control the smuggling of drugs, guns, money, and people across the US border where it hurts (their pocketbooks).

2. Disrupting them at the source by dismantling the various elements of criminal organizations and the tools they use, rather than going after contraband or smuggled people.

3. Following the money — and denying the means through which these networks get their profits back to Mexico.

In many ways these three actions are as difficult to implement as current practices. And they require enormous patience, investments in intelligence gathering, the deployment of ample law enforcement resources (including a willingness to incur private-sector ire by verifying and interfering with large-scale money transfers), changes in both legislative and regulatory frameworks, the cooperation of state and national authorities, and greater cooperation with Mexican authorities.

These requirements are not easy, nor do they come naturally to the governmental and private-sector agencies (such as wire-transfer companies and banks) that must work together to accomplish them. Moreover, the drug and criminal cartels have several advantages: they are flush with money, can adapt their practices extremely quickly to changing circumstances, do not hesitate to abandon their contraband rather than engage the government in firefights, have the proven ability to corrupt officials at all levels on both sides of the border, employ numerous subcontractors with built-in redundancies (so as not to be easily disrupted by isolated government successes), and are as brutal as they need to be.

What Goddard proposes is a comprehensive, multilayered, and deeply cooperative anti-crime effort that uses all the tools and resources potentially available to law enforcement; has clear targets (including the bosses, money, and entire infrastructure of the cartels) and goals; and dismantles the criminal networks piece by piece. Though difficult, the potential payoff is enormous. By his own acknowledgment, the approach is bold and opportunistic. Anything less could not meet the main objective of border controls: to defeat those activities that cause a receiving society the greatest harm.

---

28 Terry Goddard, *How to Fix a Broken Border: A Three Part Series* (Washington, DC: Immigration Policy Center, 2011–12), www.immigrationpolicy.org/perspectives/how-fix-broken-border-three-part-series.

IV. Perverse Consequences and Policy Feedbacks

In adopting policies and practices to combat terrorism, smuggling and trafficking, illegal migration, drug trafficking, and even asylum abuses, states face a basic dilemma: policies in any one area have perverse, regrettable, and often unintended, consequences and feedbacks. Smuggling and the multiple forms of trafficking are in some ways both the cause and the effect of "harder" border controls. States increase the number of border guards, spend more money on technology designed to protect the border and detect false documents, cooperate with like-minded states to prevent the travel of likely terrorists and unwanted migrants, use interdiction at sea and at international airports, and apply a wide variety of deterrence measures such as visas and carrier sanctions to prevent illegal migration. Yet by making irregular migration more difficult, these measures indirectly push unauthorized migrants into the hands of smugglers and traffickers. In a vicious cycle, making migration more difficult and expensive raises the risks of smuggling, which in turn raises both the costs and profits, and thus lures sophisticated criminal organizations with large resources. Their involvement then makes smuggling more difficult to stop.

Border policies also have peripheral effects, both domestic and international in scope. For example, reinforcement of the US-Mexico border has increased the level of "permanent" immigration into the United States by, in effect, "locking people in," both because of the increased cost and the higher danger of crossing the border. To escape detection, meanwhile, immigrants make crossings at more remote and dangerous places in the desert,[29] resulting in more than 400 deaths per year. At the global scale, efforts by one state to secure its borders can divert migrants to other states. When Germany, for instance, ended a right to asylum in 1993, there was almost immediately a sharp uptick in asylum applications to the United Kingdom. The relatively successful closing down of entry routes to Spain, Malta, and Italy in 2011 diverted illegal flows to Greece in a truly dramatic fashion.[30] In the area of trafficking, any successful effort to block an entry route inevitably leads traffickers to probe other, weaker entry points.

Such dilemmas will never be fully resolved, as they inhere in the policy area itself; but a number of recommendations, outlined in the final section, may limit them.

---

29 David A. Shirk, "US Immigration and Border Security" (paper presented at the Migration Policy Institute/Munk School for Global Affairs conference on The Politics and Policy of Border Security, March 22-23, 2012): 19.
30 See "Illegal Immigration Emerges as New Crisis for Greece—And EU," *Wall Street Journal*, September 15, 2012.

V. Policy Recommendations

Like immigration policy generally, the conditions of borders cannot be separated from the broader legal economic, social, and political environment. Successful states — those with prosperous economies; an unshakable commitment to the rule of law, and resulting high levels of trust between governments and peoples; and vigilance against corruption in the police, bureaucracy, and judiciary — will, all things being equal, find it easier to control borders. Put another way, weak states cannot have strong borders, and states will not get border policy right unless they get their institutions right. Proper border policy depends on low levels of corruption, effective police and border-control forces, and successful coordination both among responsible agencies and with like-minded states. In this regard, effective coordination among strong institutions and agencies is the ultimate "force multiplier" that makes borders strong and anti-crime efforts effective. A state with a strong economy, judiciary, bureaucracy, police force, and leverage in international relations (particularly bilateral and regional relations) will find it much easier to secure its borders. Where the state has not rooted out corruption or built reliable border infrastructure, as is the case in Central America's Northern Triangle and in Eastern Europe,[31] it will be impossible to create effective border-control arrangements. This means, in short, that the best border-control policies cannot overcome the shortcomings of weak states. It also means that wealthy and stable states can indirectly secure their own borders by helping other countries secure their states. This formulation has the following four implications.

A. Focus on Development, Not Just Borders

Rather than narrowly focusing international efforts in the area of immigration policy on technology transfers and border infrastructure, the focus should be on assisting weak states (or states that find themselves in transition) in strengthening the rule of law and public institutions, tackling corruption, building up national judiciaries, and training reliable police forces and border guards. Doing so will have positive effects for border policy: strong states and successful societies have better borders. To paraphrase Robert Frost, good neighbors make good fences.

B. Work Both Bilaterally and Regionally

It is almost banal to call for international cooperation, but effective border management depends on it. Different types of countries require

---

[31] See Chapter 3 in this volume, Ralph Espach and Daniel Haering, "Border Insecurity in Central America's Northern Triangle;" see Chapter 4 in this volume, Louise Shelley, "Human Smuggling and Trafficking into Europe: A Comparative Perspective."

different arrangements. Wealthy receiving countries with solid governance structures, for example, can exchange information and cooperate over the implementation of border-control policies on multiple levels: technology exchange such as biometric passports and fraud-resistant visas, shared databases on criminals, and on-the-ground cooperation in all matters involving preclearance. The European Union and the United States have made considerable progress in this area since 9/11.[32] Within the European Union itself, the European Council has adopted large numbers of directives on the reception, complementary protection, and housing of asylum seekers, as well as a Blue Card designed to create broad common standards on skilled migrants. In 2005 the Council also established the European Agency for the Management of Operational Cooperation at the External Borders of the European Union (FRONTEX), which is tasked with coordinating operational cooperation in managing external borders, assisting in the training of border guards, carrying out risk analysis, providing technical and operational assistance, and coordinating joint return.[33] (Whenever considering EU cooperation, however, it is important to reflect on the extent to which the European Union, as a sui generis organization that developed out of a particular European experience of war and genocide, can offer lessons to states without this history. We can probably learn more from European–North American cooperation than intra-EU cooperation).

It may be worth making one comment on venue and approach. If international cooperation is to be effective, it is best that it be taken out of the public eye and depoliticized.[34] The more public discussions of border management are, the more likely journalists, nationalists, and even well-intentioned advocates will frighten politicians into retreating to the policy status quo.

C. Continue to Expand Border Controls in High-Traffic Areas

There has been much criticism of DHS' increased spending on enforcement, but the results — in terms of greater border control — have been significant. This is not the time to pull back from such investments.

---

32 Demetrios G. Papademetriou and Elizabeth Collett, *A New Architecture for Border Management* (Washington, DC: Migration Policy Institute, 2011), www.migrationpolicy.org/pubs/borderarchitecture.pdf.
33 See Chapter 6 in this volume, Elizabeth Collett, *Faltering Schengen Cooperation? The Challenges to Maintaining a Stable System*.
34 See Randall Hansen, *Interstate Cooperation: Europe and Central Asia* (Geneva: International Organization for Migration [IOM], 2004); IOM, "The Berne Initiative. Managing Migration through International Cooperation: The International Agenda for Migration Management" (Berne II Conference, December 16-17, 2004), www.iom.int/jahia/webdav/site/myjahia-site/shared/shared/mainsite/policy_and_research/berne/Berne_II_Chairmans_Summary.pdf; IOM, "An Assessment of the Principal Regional Consultative Processes on Migration," *IOM Migration Research Series* No. 38 (Geneva: IOM, 2010) [This is a 50-page policy report sent to some 125 governments around the world].

Progress is also being made in other areas, which, over time, is likely to translate into fewer, and perhaps smarter, investments at US borders. Risk-management methodologies are beginning to take hold, an appreciation of the trade and economic benefits of a well-functioning border are now much higher on the agenda, and conversations — *and action* — on rethinking border controls (protecting the common North American space through smarter policies and investments in the area's external borders) are showing promise, most obviously in the US-Canada relationship, but also in the US-Mexico one. Understanding how to best protect borders will take time, but the initial effort has already gone further than many expected. As ever, however, policymakers must be aware of diversionary effects: smugglers might well target Canadian borders in response to any loosening of Canada-US controls.

D. Expand "Remote-Control" Immigration

Although unpopular with activists, there is ample evidence that expanding borders outwards works. The case of asylum seekers in Germany and Britain is instructive. In response to a sharp increase in asylum seekers in the 1990s and 2000s, both states did everything they could to push the border outwards (through carrier sanctions, visa regimes, declaring airports international zones, and fast-track procedures) and managed to sharply reduce the pressure. And as the United States has learned, such expansion is also less socially divisive than strengthening internal controls, such as through laws delegating immigration enforcement powers to the police, schools, and local bureaucrats. One critical danger of inside control, as experienced in the United States when 287(g) agreements authorized local police to take on federal immigration powers,[35] is that if immigrant communities come to fear the authorities, then the regular business of police work will become much more difficult, since people will be less willing to report crimes and communicate with law enforcement.

Critics of both sorts of policies abound. Virginie Guiraudon for instance, argues that:

> *Whether remote control consists of forcing airline companies to scrutinize their passengers' passports and visas for their validity, enticing neighboring countries to guard their own 'frontiers of poverty' (Freudenstein 2000, 172-3) or establishing 'anomalous zones' (Neuman 1996) such as extraterritorial waiting rooms in airports or offshore 'safe havens,' the goal is the same. The measures aim at preventing unwanted migrants from accessing the system of legal protection and the asylum process, thereby avoiding the domestic and international legal norms that stand in the*

---

35   Randy Capps, Marc R. Rosenblum, Cristina Rodriguez, and Muzaffar Chishti, *Delegation and Divergence: A Study of 287(g) State and Local Immigration Enforcement* (Washington, DC: Migration Policy Institute, 2011), www.migrationpolicy.org/pubs/287g-divergence.pdf.

way of restricting migration flows. This strategy, which operates before the border, also allows for less control at the point of entry itself, thus facilitating the movement of inhabitants of the first world, tourists and businessmen.[36]

Guiraudon is right, but she takes a critic's liberty, without acknowledging the deeper reason for states' insistence on jealously guarding their borders: the difficulty of securing return. In all countries, deportation only touches a minority of unauthorized migrants and failed asylum seekers. This is true even of the United States, which is currently deporting a peak 400,000 per year. The United States has probably gone as far as it can go, as it is not and will not become the sort of society that drags 11 million crying and screaming people to waiting vans and airplanes, as images are broadcast around the world on CNN. Contrary to the pronouncements of some anti-immigration activists that many will "self-deport," the vast majority of illegally resident immigrants in the United States will not leave voluntarily. For liberal states, deportation is expensive; time-consuming, given judicial activism and legal appeals; and raises popular opposition. It also creates a climate of suspicion and fear. Short of doing nothing in the face of spiraling asylum applications and illegal migration, the alternative to "remote-control" immigration is vastly expanded deportation and societal chaos of one sort or another.

VI. Conclusions

In summary, a complex and varied relationship exists between borders and other policy areas on the one hand, and borders and security on the other. Securing a border involves much more that controlling it: the nature of institutions, social norms, corruption, global forces outside the country, and the ever-present contest with trafficking and smuggling networks all have a direct impact on a state's ability to control its borders. In this chapter, we have focused on the steps that states have been taking to prevent unwanted migrants and contraband from reaching and crossing their borders, and have assumed that states' interests in these goals are legitimate. We have also argued that securing borders is basic both to state sovereignty *and* migrant human rights, as the alternative to expanded control at the border is not less control, but rather expanded and intrusive internal controls. The former is widely recognized; the latter rarely is. Finally, we have reviewed a number of policy proposals for successful border security and made four recommendations:

1. Ensure that receiving states focus on positively affecting the legal and public institutions, economic development, border capacities, and levels of corruption in sending countries, since weak states cannot have effective border policies.

---

36 Guiraudon, "Enlisting Third Parties in Border Control."

2. Expand bilateral and regional cooperation.

3. Increase physical border enforcement in states where it is sparse.

4. Continue to expand border control outwards.

All the while, it is important to recognize that all efforts of border control can have perverse consequences that negatively affect migrant welfare and — often at the same time — make the task of controlling borders more difficult still.

Some of these policy recommendations will meet understandable opposition. As with all migration policy choices, options need to be considered in comparison with other alternatives. Given the robust legal, moral, and economic constraints on expanded deportation, and the imperatives of protection against the potential for terrorism and unwanted and dangerous contraband, states have little choice but to invest their efforts in making borders as secure from unwanted crossings as possible. At the end of the day, immigration policy is not about writing a new theory of normative justice, but choosing the lesser evil.

Works Cited

Barnes, Robert. 2012. Supreme Court upholds key part of Arizona law for now, strikes down other provisions. *Washington Post*, June 25, 2012. http://articles.washingtonpost.com/2012-06-25/politics/35461864_1_immigration-decision-arizona-law-illegal-immigrants.

Brick, Kate. 2011. *Regularizations in the European Union: The Contentious Policy Tool*. Washington, DC: Migration Policy Institute. www.migrationpolicy.org/pubs/EURegularization-Insight.pdf.

Capps, Randy, Marc R. Rosenblum, Cristina Rodriguez, and Muzaffar Chishti. 2011. *Delegation and Divergence: A Study of 287(g) State and Local Immigration Enforcement*. Washington, DC: Migration Policy Institute. www.migrationpolicy.org/pubs/287g-divergence.pdf.

Collett, Elizabeth. 2013. Faltering Schengen Cooperation? The Challenges to Maintaining a Stable System. In *Managing Borders in an Increasingly Borderless World*, eds. Randall Hansen and Demetrios G. Papademetriou. Washington, DC: Migration Policy Institute.

Dawson, Laura. 2012. The Canada-U.S. Border Action Plan: This Time It's For Real, Charlie Brown. In *A Safe and Smart Border: The Ongoing Quest in U.S.-Canada Relations*. One Issue Two Voices series, issue 15, The Wilson Center, September 2012. www.wilsoncenter.org/sites/default/files/CI_120828_One%20Issue%20Two%20Voices%2015_FINAL.pdf.

Espach, Ralph and Daniel Haering. 2013. Border Insecurity in Central America's Northern Triangle. In *Managing Borders in an Increasingly Borderless World*, eds. Randall Hansen and Demetrios G. Papademetriou. Washington, DC: Migration Policy Institute.

Goddard, Terry. 2011–12. *How to Fix a Broken Border: A Three Part Series*. Washington, DC: Immigration Policy Center. www.immigrationpolicy.org/perspectives/how-fix-broken-border-three-part-series.

Guiraudon, Virginie. 2006. Enlisting Third Parties in Border Control: A Comparative Study of its Causes and Consequences. In *Borders and Security Governance*, eds. Marina Caparini and Otwin Marenin. Geneva: Geneva Centre for the Democratic Control of Armed Forces.

Hansen, Randall. 2004. *Interstate Cooperation: Europe and Central Asia*. Geneva: International Organization for Migration.

Hoefer, Michael, Nancy Rytina, and Bryan Baker. 2012. *Estimates of the Unauthorized Immigrant Population Residing in the United States: January 2011*. Washington, DC: Department of Homeland Security, Office of Immigration Statistics. www.dhs.gov/sites/default/files/publications/ois_ill_pe_2011.pdf.

International Labor Organization (ILO). 2005. *A Global Alliance against Forced Labour*. Geneva: International Labor Office. www.ilo.org/public/english/standards/relm/ilc/ilc93/pdf/rep-i-b.pdf.

International Organization on Migration (IOM). 2010. An Assessment of the Principal Regional Consultative Processes on Migration. *IOM Migration Research Series* No. 38. Geneva: IOM.

_____. The Berne Initiative. Managing Migration through International Cooperation: The International Agenda for Migration Management. Berne II Conference, December 16-17, 2004. www.iom.int/jahia/webdav/site/myjahiasite/shared/shared/mainsite/policy_and_research/berne/Berne_II_Chairmans_Summary.pdf.

Lahav, Gallya and Virginie Guiraudon. 2000. Comparative Perspectives on Border Control: Away from the Border and Outside the State. In *The Wall around the West: State Borders and Immigration Controls in North America and Europe*, eds. Peter Andreas and Timothy Snyder. Lanham, MD: Rowman and Littlefield Publishers.

Laqueur, Walter. 1988. *The Age of Terrorism*. London: Little Brown and Company.

Marenin, Otwin. 2006. Democratic Oversight and Border Management: Principles, Complexity, and Agency Interests. In *Borders and Security Governance*, eds. Marina Caparini and Otwin Marenin. Geneva: Geneva Centre for the Democratic Control of Armed Forces.

Morehouse, Christal and Michael Blomfield. 2011. *Irregular Migration in Europe*. Washington, DC: Migration Policy Institute. www.migrationpolicy.org/pubs/tcmirregularmigration.pdf.

Neumayer, Eric. Asylum Recognition Rates in Western Europe: Their Determinants, Variation, and Lack of Convergence. *Journal of Conflict Resolution* 49, no. 1 (2005): 43–66.

Papademetriou, Demetrios G. and Elizabeth Collett. 2011. *A New Architecture for Border Management*. Washington, DC: Migration Policy Institute. www.migrationpolicy.org/pubs/borderarchitecture.pdf.

Passel, Jeffrey. 2005. *Unauthorized Migrants: Numbers and Characteristics*. Washington, DC: Pew Research Center. http://pewhispanic.org/files/reports/46.pdf.

Perl, Raphael, F. 2006. *International Drug Trade and US Foreign Policy* (Washington, DC: Congressional Research Service): 2-5. https://opencrs.com/document/RL33582/.

Pollard, Niklas. 2005. UN report puts world's illicit drug trade at estimated $321b. Reuters, June 30, 2005.

Riley, K. Jack. 2005. Border Control. In *The McGraw-Hill Homeland Security Handbook*, ed. David Kamien. Columbus: McGraw-Hill.

Saha, K. C. 2009. *Smuggling of Migrants from India to Europe and in Particular to UK: A Study on Tamil Nadu*. New Delhi: United Nations Office on Drugs and Crime (UNODC). www.unodc.org/documents/human-trafficking/Smuggling_of_Migrants_from_India.pdf.

Schwartz, John. 2012. Supreme Court Decision on Arizona Immigration Law. *New York Times*, June 26, 2012. www.nytimes.com/interactive/2012/06/26/us/scotus-immigrationlaw-analysis.html?_r=0.

Shelley, Louise. 2010. *2013*. Human Smuggling and Trafficking into Europe: A Comparative Perspective. In Managing Borders in an Increasingly Borderless World, eds. Randall Hansen and Demetrios G. Papademetriou. Washington, DC: Migration Policy Institute.

Shirk, David A. 2012. US Immigration and Border Security. Paper presented at the Migration Policy Institute/Munk School for Global Affairs conference on "The Politics and Policy of Border Security," March 22-23, 2012.

United Nations General Assembly. 2000. *Protocol against the Smuggling of Migrants by Land, Sea, and Air, Supplementing the United Nations Convention against Transnational Organized Crime.* www.refworld.org/docid/479dee062.html.

_____. 2009. *Smuggling of Migrants.* Vienna: UNODC. www.unodc.org/documents/human-trafficking/Migrant_Smuggling/09-81206_English_eBook.pdf.

_____. 2011. *World Drug Report 2011.* New York: UNODC. www.unodc.org/documents/data-and-analysis/WDR2011/World_Drug_Report_2011_ebook.pdf.

CHAPTER 2

CHALLENGES TO THE COMMON EUROPEAN ASYLUM SYSTEM:

THE DUBLIN RULES UNDER JUDICIAL PRESSURE

Kay Hailbronner
Universität Konstanz

I. Introduction

Asylum law, traditionally a key expression of national sovereignty, has become a major field of legislation in the European Union (EU). Just as EU Member States have ceded considerable autonomy in their border-control policies by participating in the Schengen system,[1] they have also taken part in a well-articulated common strategy for granting asylum. Recent years have seen a proliferation of EU lawmaking in this field, leaving Member States little flexibility over asylum policy.

Nonetheless, national implementation of EU policies is lagging. The success of these policies is increasingly threatened by the inability or unwillingness of some Member States to comply with the common commitment to providing every asylum seeker a fair and efficient asylum procedure. According to the rules of the Dublin Regulation, the state through which an asylum seeker first entered the European Union is usually the state that is responsible for the processing the claim. However, the EU Member States with external borders (the "front states") complain about the lack of a burden-sharing system that assigns sufficient responsibility for asylees to other Member States.

---

1   See Chapter 6 of this volume, Elizabeth Collett, "Faltering Schengen Cooperation? The Challenges to Maintaining a Stable System."

Insufficient application of EU law in some states has provoked the intervention of a progressive international jurisprudence: the European Court of Human Rights has attempted to compel Member States to apply EU asylum law more rigorously. And the difficulties of applying the high standards of EU law under the pressure of spontaneous refugee movements have created new challenges. These problems have resulted in a partial suspension of the Dublin system of assigning responsibility for processing asylum claims.

II. The Common European Asylum System

A. *The Foundation of the Common European Asylum System*

Asylum and immigration policy has become a matter of intergovernmental cooperation among EU Member States. The Dublin Convention of 1990 was the first binding legal instrument in asylum law. It was signed alongside the Schengen Convention, which abolished internal border controls and set a common visa policy among its signatories. The Dublin Convention was one of the "compensatory mechanisms" for this loss of control — it set rules for processing asylum applications, assigning exclusive responsibility to the state through which the applicant first entered the European Union.

Following the signing of the Dublin Convention, the competences of the European Union were gradually enlarged with the entry into force of the Treaty of Maastricht in 1993 and the Treaty of Amsterdam in 1999. The Treaty of Amsterdam ushered in the first phase of directives and regulations of the Common European Asylum System. In the following years, the Dublin Convention became the Dublin Regulation, and Eurodac — the European fingerprint database for identifying asylum seekers — was adopted. Together, these regulations form the Dublin system.

The Dublin system is a cornerstone of the Common European Asylum System. It has now been extended beyond the scope of EU Member States to associated states, including Norway and Iceland in 2001, and Switzerland and Liechtenstein in 2008. The basic objective of the Dublin Regulation is to avoid multiple or successive applications for asylum. Since asylum is intended to grant protection against political persecution as defined by the Geneva Convention, a refugee should not be permitted to apply for asylum in more than one Dublin Member State.

In 2005, the first phase of the Common European Asylum System ended with the adoption of the Asylum Procedures Directive, the fifth piece of legislation arising from the asylum-related agenda of the Amsterdam

Treaty. The directive established standards for granting and withdrawing refugee status, and dealt with procedures related to border activities, detention, interviews, and legal assistance.

The Hague Programme of 2004 laid the basis for further development of Common European Asylum System in a second phase of EU lawmaking. The regulations of the second phase updated the main measures set forth in the first phase, including the Dublin system regulations and the procedures governing the processing of asylum claims and the treatment of claimants.

The Common European Asylum System was explicitly introduced by the Lisbon Treaty, signed in 2007 and entered into force in 2009.[2] The system introduced a uniform status of refugee, subsidiary protection, and temporary protection recognized throughout the European Union. It also embraced common procedures for granting and withdrawing asylum or subsidiary protection status, standards for the reception of applicants for asylum or subsidiary protection, and partnership and cooperation with third countries.

Many of these points had already been addressed in existing EU directives and regulations, including the rules on temporary protection for displaced persons, and the criteria and mechanisms for determining whether a third-country national qualifies for refugee or subsidiary protection. However, these directives only set out minimum standards, which Member States were permitted to deviate from in favor of an asylum seeker. They were also established on the basis of the principle of unanimity, which required substantial concessions to be made, resulting in some vague formulations and opt-out provisions.[3] This changed with the entry into force of the Lisbon Treaty, which provides for qualified majority decisions and joint decision-making between the European Parliament and the European Council. Qualified majority voting has meant that, for the first time, national objections based on the desire to maintain existing asylum or immigration legislation can be overruled.

---

2   European Union (EU), *Treaty of Lisbon Amending the Treaty on European Union and the Treaty Establishing the European Community*, 2007/C 306/01, December 13, 2007, Article 78 TFEU. For the development of EU asylum legislation, see Steve Peers, *EU Justice and Home Affairs Law*, 3rd edition (Oxford: Oxford University Press, 2011).

3   The provisions on safe third countries illustrate this point. According to Article 46 of the Asylum Procedures Directive, Member States may refuse to examine an asylum application if a competent authority has established that an applicant is safe. However, the provision leaves it open whether this may be in accordance with the Geneva Convention since Member States are subject to the principle of *nonrefoulement* and rules providing for exceptions from the application of this article for humanitarian or political reasons or for reasons of public international law. The extent to which Member States are obliged under public international law to provide for a safe third-country rule without undermining the presumption of safety is unclear. See Council of the European Union, "Council Directive 2005/85/EC on minimum standards on procedures in Member States for granting and withdrawing refugee status," December 1, 2005, EUR-Lex L 326/13, http://eur-lex.europa.eu/LexUriServ/LexUriServ.do?uri=OJ:L:2005:326:0013:0034:EN:PDF.

The Lisbon Treaty also replaces the minimum standards in the existing directives with a set of common standards, and removes disparities between Member States in relation to granting protection and to the form that protection takes. The basic idea is that the Common European Asylum System will rank as a primary EU-law concept to allow a systematic approach to the asylum acquis where all components are harmonized, leaving no space for gaps or inconsistencies.

B. Balancing Sovereign Rights and Shared Responsibility

Despite their commitment to the aims of Common European Asylum System, EU Member States have found it difficult to give up their sovereign rights to control the entry of third-country nationals into their territories. This tension between the desire for sovereignty and the need to share responsibilities is illustrated by a 2001 directive on minimum standards for granting temporary protection in the event of a mass influx of displaced persons, and on measures promoting a balance of efforts between Member States receiving such persons.[4] The directive is an interesting piece of legislation as it reflects the difficulties in achieving a balance of interests between the sovereign right to decide admission and some kind of European solidarity in a situation of mass refugee movements. The purpose of the directive is to provide protection to displaced persons who have been victims of systematic or generalized violations of human rights, or have fled areas of armed conflict in the European Union. It has, however, not yet been applied and perhaps may never be of practical importance.

The directive provides for a procedure in a situation of a mass influx that can be established by a Council decision on the basis of qualified majority voting. However, this does not result in obligations on the part of all Member States participating in an admission scheme. The Council decision only introduces temporary protection rights for displaced persons in Member States that have chosen to receive persons eligible for temporary protection. Member States are required to indicate their capacity to receive persons (in figures or in general terms), and can indicate additional reception capacity by notifying the Council and the Commission. The Council may also recommend additional support for the Member States affected, but there is no competence to distribute displaced persons according to some kind of a burden-sharing mechanism. The system therefore has been described as a system of "double pledging." This means that although the directive uses the term "community solidarity," EU Member States must agree to the adoption of the

---

4 Council of the European Union, "Council Directive 2001/55/EC on minimum standards for giving temporary protection in the event of a mass influx of displaced persons and on measures promoting a balance of efforts between Member States in such persons and bearing the consequences thereof," July 20, 2001, EUR-Lex L 212/12, http://eur-lex.europa.eu/LexUriServ/LexUriServ.do?uri=OJ:L:2001:212:0012:0023:EN:PDF. See also Achilles Skordas,"Commentary," in *EU Immigration and Asylum Law*, ed. Kay Hailbronner (Oxford: Hart Publishing, 2010).

resolution establishing the system in a particular situation, and explicitly accept its application to the respective Member State.[5]

Illegal immigration and security concerns have no weight under the Dublin system if an EU Member State can be identified as responsible for processing a claim for international protection under the rules of the qualification directive. This means that the responsible Member State is obliged to admit the applicant and to grant all rights according to the conditions of the reception directive[6] and the asylum procedures directive.[7] The procedures directive allows for accelerated procedures in the case of manifestly abusive or unfounded claims, but does not allow restrictions on admission, irrespective of numbers and the situation in which a claim for admission is filed. This creates new challenges, particularly for the "front states."

C. The Main Pillars of the Common European Asylum System

A core pillar of the Common European Asylum System is the harmonization of the criteria for recognition as a refugee or a person entitled to "subsidiary protection,"[8] including rules on cessation or exclusion of persons presenting a security danger. This is in contrast to the first generation of EU directives, which had left scope for discretion in applying EU law. The new generation of directives in the area of asylum procedures, reception conditions, and qualification criteria will harmonize national legislation and make substantial steps toward a uniform status.

However, a uniform status requires equal application of the rules, not just equal rules. In this context the jurisprudence of the European Court of Justice becomes increasingly important for a harmonized application of the directives through national courts. The European Court of Justice has already passed some important decisions with regard to the qualification directive, for instance, on the qualification

---

5   Council of the European Union, "Council Directive 2001/55/EC on minimum standards for giving temporary protection," Article 25, paragraph 1. Also see for legislating history, Skordas, "Commentary."
6   Council of the European Union, "Council Directive 2003/9/EC on Laying Down Minimum Standards for the Reception of Asylum Seekers," January 27, 2003, EUR-Lex L 31/18, http://eur-lex.europa.eu/LexUriServ/LexUriServ.do?uri=OJ:L:2003:031:0018:0025:EN:PDF.
7   Council of the European Union, "Council Directive 2005/85/EC on minimum standards on procedures in Member States for granting and withdrawing refugee status."
8   Subsidiary protection covers applications for international protection, inter alia based upon torture or inhuman treatment or indiscriminate violence in situations of international or internal armed conflict. See Article 15 of European Parliament and Council of the European Union, "Directive 2011/95/ EU on standards for the qualification of third-country nationals or stateless persons as beneficiaries of international protection, for a uniform status for refugees or for persons eligible for subsidiary protection, and for the content of the protection granted," December 13, 2011, EUR-Lex L 337/9, http://eur-lex.europa.eu/LexUriServ/LexUriServ.do?uri=OJ:L:2011:337:0009:0026:EN:PDF.

for subsidiary protection. Article 15 of the directive defines subsidiary protection inter alia as a "serious and individual threat to a civilian's life or person by reason of indiscriminate violence in situations of international or internal armed conflict."[9] The requirement of an "individual threat" had been included to respond to the concerns of some EU Member States about an uncontrollable influx of war or civil war refugees. When the question came before European Court of Justice in a landmark case, the court decided that Article 15 does not require an applicant to show evidence that he or she is specifically targeted because of factors particular to his or her personal circumstances. The court also affirmed that the existence of a threat can be considered to be established where the degree of indiscriminate violence characterizing the armed conflict reaches such a high level that there are substantial grounds for believing that a civilian, solely on account of his presence in the territory, would face a real risk of being subject to that threat.[10]

Another pillar of the Common European Asylum System is the provision of partnership and cooperation with third countries for the purpose of managing inflows of people applying for asylum or subsidiary or temporary protection. The Commission has repeatedly pointed to the need for concluding partnership agreements setting out rules governing admission of qualified migrants, rules controlling irregular transit migration, and, eventually, asylum processing outside of the European Union. However, such efforts have not yet produced substantial results. The dilemma confronting the European Union is illustrated by the agreement between Italy and Libya providing for the return of "boat refugees" to Libya.[11] This was declared incompatible with Italy's obligations under Article 3 and 13, and Article 4 of Protocol No. 4 of

---

9 Council of the European Union, "Council Directive 2004/83/EC on minimum standards for the qualification and status of third-country nationals or stateless persons as refugees or as persons who otherwise need international protection and the content of the protection granted," Article 15, EUR-Lex L 304/12, April 29, 2004, http://eur-lex.europa.eu/LexUriServ/LexUriServ.do?uri=OJ:L:2004:304:0012:0023:EN:PDF.

10 *Meki Elgafaji and Noor Elgafaji v. Staatssecretaris van Justitie*, C-465/07 ECR I-921 (European Court of Justice, 2009), http://curia.europa.eu/juris/celex.jsf?celex=62007CJ0465&lang1=en&type=NOT&ancre. See also Hailbronner, "Asylum Law"; Roland Bank, "Das Elgafaji-Urteil des EuGH und seine Bedeutung für den Schutz von Personen, die vor bewaffneten Konflikten fliehen," *Neue Zeitschrift für Verwaltungsrecht* 11 (2009): 695-99; and Federal Administrative Court (Germany), case no. 10 C 11/07, May 29, 2005, BVerwGE 131, 186, para. 30 ff. Accessed from European Database of Asylum Law, www.asylumlawdatabase.eu/en/case-law/germany-%E2%80%93-federal-administrative-court-29-may-2008-10-c-1107#content.

11 The agreement between Italy and Libya was concluded on December 29, 2007 and supplemented by an additional protocol on February 4, 2009 providing for repatriation of clandestine immigrants. For details, see *Hirsi Jamaa and others v. Italy* 27765/09 (European Court of Human Rights, 2012), http://hudoc.echr.coe.int/sites/eng/pages/search.aspx?i=001-109231#.

the European Convention on Human Rights (ECHR).[12] Once again, this raises new questions about the functioning of an asylum system based upon cooperation with third states.

III. Policy Challenges

The European Union is a major receiving region for asylum seekers. There were over 330,000 asylum applications received by EU states in 2012, an increase of about 30,000 from 2011.[13] Major recipients of asylum applications in 2012 were Germany (77,540) and France (60,560), followed by Sweden (43,265), the United Kingdom (28,175) and Belgium (28,105).[14] Greece and Italy received 9,575 and 15,715 applications respectively in 2012, which did not account for as large an influx as one might expect, given that they are "front states."[15] Major countries of origin in 2012 were Afghanistan (26,250), Syria (23,510), Russia (23,360), Pakistan (19,290), and Serbia (18,900).[16] Smaller but still substantial numbers of applicants were from Somalia, Iran, Iraq, Georgia, and Kosovo.

Some Member States receive inflows primarily from a single country. For instance, Poland received 57 percent of its applicants in 2012 from Russia; Lithuania, 48 percent from Georgia; Bulgaria, 32 percent from Syria and 23 percent from Iraq; Latvia, 51 percent from Georgia; and Hungary, 41 percent from Afghanistan.[17]

In addition to application rates, Eurostat also records the number of decisions and the recognition rate. In 2012, 268,500 applications were decided. Of these, about 73 percent (196,920 applications) were rejected and nearly 14 percent (37,245 applicants) were recognized as refugees. An additional 27,920 applicants (10 percent) received subsidiary protection, and 6,415 were granted a residence permit on national humanitarian grounds.[18] This suggests that a large volume of illegal migration is processed through the EU asylum system. However, third-country nationals arriving illegally without registering as asylum seekers are not counted in these statistics. The numbers of

---

12   Article 3 of the European Convention on Human Rights provides for protection against inhuman or degrading treatment or punishment, Article 13 guarantees a remedy, and Article 4 of Protocol No. 4 prohibits collective expulsion.
13   Alexandros Bitoulas, "Asylum applicants and first instance decisions on asylum applications," Eurostat, Data in Focus (Brussels: European Union, May 2013), http://epp.eurostat.ec.europa.eu/cache/ITY_OFFPUB/KS-QA-13-005/EN/KS-QA-13-005-EN.PDF.
14   Ibid., 4.
15   It has to be noted, however, that a substantial number of third-country nationals are not registered in these countries, either for administrative reasons or because of poor asylum conditions, which means that no claim is made.
16   Alexandros Bitoulas, "Asylum applicants and first instance decisions on asylum applications."
17   Ibid.
18   Ibid.

migrants arriving in the 28 EU Member States without authorization do not appear in the statistics of the Member States, nor in the Eurodac databases used for registering persons applying for refugee status.

With the abolition of internal border controls, the European Union has become more attractive to migrants. Irregular and unidentified migration flows, coupled with successful asylum claims and the great difficulty states face in returning unsuccessful asylum seekers, all greatly limit the capacity of states to control migration. Preventing uncontrolled migration within the European Union will only be possible with a functioning system of exclusive responsibility, which requires mutual trust in the fairness and efficiency of the system. The application of the Dublin rules is therefore intrinsically connected to the aim of controlling illegal migration into the European Union.

The goal of providing procedural fairness and justice to persons in need of international protection is difficult to reconcile with the public interest in making rapid and firm decisions and removing persons who do not qualify for protection. Rules on exclusive competence do not help much in this regard. Uniform EU rules on receiving and processing pose new challenges in the face of the diverse geographical and economic characteristics of EU Member States. For example, Member States with external borders clearly encounter different problems in controlling migration flows than those with few or no external borders.

A further security challenge faced by EU Member States in applying the common rules on asylum applications concerns the admission of applicants involved in terrorist activities or serious crimes. The qualification directive, in accordance with the Geneva Conventions, permits Member States to exclude applicants from protection on the grounds that they present a serious danger to security or public order.[19] But it does not allow countries to refuse to admit an asylum seeker. The obligation to admit is absolute, under the jurisprudence of the European Court of Human Rights, if there are serious reasons to suspect that an applicant may face the danger of inhuman treatment. Such a risk may emanate from the government of the sending state, or from persons or groups who are not public officials. The extension of the application of this obligation to coast guards operating within Frontex, the European border management agency, will open up new challenges to the application of these high EU standards.

---

19 Council of the Euroepan Union, Directive 2004/83/EC on minimum standards for the qualification and status of third-country nationals or stateless persons as refugees, Article 12.

IV. Implementation of the Common European Asylum System

A. The Difficulties of Assigning Responsibility

The Dublin system requires all applicants to have access to a refugee status determination procedure in only one of the Member States, and mandates that all Member States participating in the system be "safe." Safety is defined by the principle of *nonrefoulement*[20] (not returning a person to a persecuting state) as well as treatment in accordance with basic human rights, in particular the right to be treated humanely according to Article 3 of the ECHR. Third-country nationals using asylum procedures for "forum shopping" will therefore be sent back to the responsible asylum state. The Dublin Regulation also sets out the procedures, time limits, and formalities of asylum applications in detail.

The Dublin system constitutes an essential part of the Common European Asylum System and as such is intrinsically connected to the harmonization project. All EU Member States are obliged to apply the minimum standards of the directive on the reception of asylum seekers[21] as well as common standards on the recognition of asylum seekers laid down in the qualification directive. While the directives do not need to be binding for the Dublin Regulation to apply (because it is applicable to associated non-EU Member States), there are basic standards that have to be fulfilled in all participating states in order for a state to qualify as safe.

From the outset, the efficiency of the Dublin system was based on the assumption that travel routes could be easily identified. Asylum seekers wishing to apply for asylum in a specific EU country have an interest in hiding their travel route to avoid the country of first entry being designated the responsible country. After the Eurodac Regulation of 2000 established a database to register asylum seekers and unauthorized third-country nationals, it became easier to trace travel routes and send asylum seekers back to the competent EU Member State

---

20 The principle of nonrefoulement constitutes an essential component of asylum and international refugee protection. The essence of the principle is that a state may not oblige a person to return to a territory where he may be exposed to persecution. See United Nations High Commissioner for Refugees (UNHCR), *The Principle of Non-Refoulement as a Norm of Customary International Law. Response to the Questions Posed to UNHCR by the Federal Constitutional Court of the Federal Republic of Germany in Cases 2 BvR 1938/93, 2 BvR 1953/93, 2 BvR 1954/93*, January 31, 1994, www.refworld.org/docid/437b6db64.html.
21 Council of the European Union, "Council Directive 2003/9/EC on laying down minimum standards for the reception of asylum seekers;" and Marcus Peek, "Commentary," in *EU Immigration and Asylum Law*, ed. Kay Hailbronner (Oxford: Hart Publishing, 2010).

within the time frame required by the Dublin Regulation.[22]

But increased efficiency in tracing travel routes meant that Dublin system countries with external borders faced a higher burden than countries, such as Germany, surrounded by "safe" states. This has put pressure on some countries to avoid registering their asylum seekers. It is an open secret that some EU Member States choose not to register asylum seekers or unauthorized migrants and instead encourage them to head further north. Nonetheless, Eurodac has played an important role in identifying successive or dual asylum applications when it has been applied and has functioned effectively.

The problem is that the Dublin system has not led to a burden-sharing system. Hence, with the exception of the European Refugee Fund — designed to boost the capacity of Member States in receiving and processing refugees and displaced persons and to provide support for special projects — no distribution mechanisms have been established.[23] The numbers of registered asylum seekers have therefore remained relatively small, in spite of improved possibilities for identifying asylum seekers through travel criteria. Third-country nationals seeking to reach their destination often do not apply for asylum or do not register at all, and are sent further on so that the original receiving state can get rid of the problem.

For example, Italy developed special techniques like issuing a kind of a temporary residence permit to allow North African immigrants who had entered the European Union from Tunisia to go on to France. This resulted in France reintroducing internal border checks with Italy in April 2011 to prevent these immigrants entering the country.[24] Italy has also released asylum seekers sent back from other EU Member States within the framework of the Dublin system with the order to "voluntarily" return to their home countries even though it was likely that they would return to the EU Member State that had sent them to Italy. Switzerland has also had difficulties applying the Dublin rules to asylum applicants entering Switzerland through Italy, because Italy has made it difficult to return them.[25] These examples do not necessarily imply that the Dublin Regulation exists only on paper. But they show

---

22 Council of the European Union, "Council Regulation (EC) No 343/2003 establishing the criteria and mechanisms for determining the Member State responsible for examining an asylum application lodged in one of the Member States by a third-country national," Article 17, February 18, 2003, EUR-Lex L 50/1, http://eur-lex.europa.eu/LexUriServ/LexUriServ.do?uri=OJ:L:2003:050:0001:0010:EN:PDF.
23 See Eiko R. Thielemann, "Between Interests and Norms: Explaining Burden-Sharing in the European Union," *Journal of Refugee Studies* 16, no. 3 (2003): 253–73.
24 See Sergio Carrera, Elspeth Guild, Massimo Merlino, and Joanna Parkin, *A Race Against Solidarity: The Schengen-Regime and the Franco-Italian Affair* (Brussels: Centre for European Policy Studies, 2011), www.ceps.be/book/race-against-solidarity-schengen-regime-and-franco-italian-affair.
25 For instance, instead of transferring applicants back to Italy by way of a simple transfer on the land borders, Italy requested that Switzerland transfer them by air to Milan.

that there are substantial difficulties in applying the agreement to states with external borders.

B. The Premise of the Dublin System and the Case of Greece

The Dublin Regulation is based upon several prerequisites. The first is the assumption of migrant safety in every state participating in the system. There is also a presumption that the process for determining the responsible Member State and the subsequent transfer proceedings will be finished within a short time frame. For that reason the Dublin Regulation has been amended to speed up the proceedings. A request must be submitted within three months of the date on which an application was lodged. The Member State in question must make a decision within two months on a request to take charge. Moreover, the criteria for proof as set out in the Dublin Regulation have become easier to meet: circumstantial evidence can now be accepted where there is no formal proof.

The Dublin Regulation also provides asylum seekers with the option of challenging a transfer decision. The decision may be subject to an appeal or a review, but this does not suspend the implementation of the transfer unless national legislation explicitly allows for it. This provision has prompted a substantial number of court decisions in Germany and other countries challenging the safety of some Dublin states, in particular Greece.

The difficulties with the application of the Dublin system have been raised in judgments of the European Court of Human Rights (ECtHR) and the European Court of Justice (ECJ). The cases in question are *M.S.S. v. Belgium and Greece*[26] (dealing with the obligations of EU Member States to comply with Article 3 of the ECHR on the application of the Dublin rules) and *N.S. v. Secretary of State for the Home Department*[27] (relating to a Member State's obligations under general principles of EU Law and the Dublin Regulation). Both judgments dealt with orders of transfer to Greece of asylum seekers who had passed through Greece to other Member States. The applicants, supported by many nongovernmental organizations and the Office of the United Nations High Commissioner for Refugees (UNHCR), claimed the suspension of the Dublin system and a right of admission to the asylum procedure in the state of residence.

---

26 *M.S.S. v Belgium and Greece*, Applicant No. 30696/09 (European Court of Justice, 2011), http://ec.europa.eu/anti-trafficking/entity.action;jsessionid=hD6vRTjDbDsK7qnvQZt8 Tjy4hGMWvKqLP6WhTjM0gc0TJKXSr1Md!1062222535?path=Legislation+and+Case+L aw/Case+Law/CASE+OF+M.S.S.+v.+BELGIUM+AND+GREECE. For a detailed analysis of the consequences, see Daniel Thym, *Menschenrechtliche Feinjustierung des Dublinsystems zur Asylzuständigkeitsabgrenzung — zu den Folgewirkungen des Straßburger M.S.S. — Urteils* (Baden-Baden, Germany: Zeitschrift für Ausländerrecht und Ausländerpolitik, 2011).

27 *N.S. v. Secretary of State for the Home Department*, Case C-411/10 (European Court of Human Rights, 2011), http://eur-lex.europa.eu/LexUriServ/LexUriServ.do?uri=CELEX:6201 0CJ0411:EN:HTML. For an analysis, see Kay Hailbronner and Daniel Thym, "Vertrauen im Europäischen Asylsystem," *Neue Zeitschrift für Verwaltungsrecht* 4, No. 21 (2011).

The cases were brought forth amid an increase in numbers of asylum seekers at the Greek border due to Greece's geographical location and its inability to effectively control its borders. Both courts based their judgments on the specific situation in Greece. Ninety percent of the apprehensions for unauthorized entry into the European Union in 2010 took place in Greece; in 2008, this proportion was 50 percent.[28] According to the ECtHR, this resulted in a substantial and disproportionate burden on Greece compared to other Member States. Greece proved unable to cope with this burden, and proposed that the Dublin Regulation be amended to allow exceptions to the criterion that makes the EU Member of first entry exclusively responsible. Second, whether due to the sheer numbers of arriving immigrants or to its ineffective asylum procedure, Greece failed to fulfill EU requirements relating to the EU Reception Directive and the EU Asylum Procedure Directive. (This was in spite of substantial financial support from the European Refugee Fund). In response, national courts in various EU Member States decided to delay deportation proceedings. These orders to delay have frequently been based on reports by refugee organizations and UNHCR that concluded that neither the accommodation nor the process of submitting an asylum request were in accordance with standards for admission and humane treatment, and therefore that any transfer order would violate Article 3 of the European Convention on Human Rights (a prohibition of inhuman or degrading treatment or punishment).

Early attempts to bring the issue of safety to the Supreme Courts and ECtHR, however, failed. The court confirmed a previous judgment and a judgment of the House of Lords stating that a transfer would be in violation of the ECHR only if there was a concrete danger of refoulement to a persecuting state. But it refused to identify a "real risk" in the case of Greece. The court based its judgment on the right to seek redress against potential human-rights violations by the Greek authorities under national law and the Convention.[29] Its focus was primarily on compliance with the principle of nonrefoulement rather than on identifying the procedures and laws in each Dublin Member State.[30]

1. The *M.S.S.* Judgment

The designation of Greece as a safe country changed due to the *M.S.S.* judgment of 2011, when the ECtHR considered a Belgian transfer order against an Afghan asylum seeker who had traveled via Iran and Turkey.

---

28 Charalambos Kasimis, "Greece: Illegal Immigration in the Midst of a Crisis," *Migration Information Source*, March 2012, www.migrationinformation.org/Profiles/display.cfm?ID=884.
29 *K.R.S. v. United Kingdom*, Applicant No. 32733/08 (European Court of Human Rights, 2008), http://hudoc.echr.coe.int/sites/eng/pages/search.aspx?i=001-90500#.
30 *Regina v. Secretary of State for the Home Department Ex Parte Jogathas*, UCHL 36 (House of Lords, 2002), www.publications.parliament.uk/pa/ld199899/ldjudgmt/jd990708/obrien01.htm. See Matthias Hermann, "Commentary," in *EU Immigration and Asylum Law*, ed. Kay Hailbronner (Oxford: Hart Publishing, 2010); cf. *Canadian Council for Refugees v. Canada*, F C 1262 (Canadian Federal Court, 2007), relating to the safe third-country agreement between Canada and the United States.

The asylum seeker had entered the European Union through Greece, where he was registered by the Greek authorities, detained for a week, and issued an order to leave the country. He did not apply for asylum in Greece but went on to Belgium. The court found that the subsequent transfer by Belgium back to Greece violated the right of an effective remedy, on the basis of a variety of reports on the Greek asylum situation by refugee organizations and UNHCR.[31] The applicant had argued that Belgium was obliged to examine his application for asylum in derogation from the general rules on the competent Dublin state under Article 3, Paragraph 2 of the Dublin Regulation.

This clause, sometimes defined as the "sovereignty clause," gives each Member State the right to examine an application even if such examination is not its responsibility under the Dublin Regulation. In such a case the Member State concerned becomes the responsible state. The court relied upon numerous reports and materials describing the deficiencies of the Greek asylum procedure, and on reports that the applicant's conditions of detention under Articles 3 and 13 of the ECHR and his living conditions in Greece were degrading.[32] The court concluded that the general situation was known to the Belgian authorities, and that they were therefore violating their obligations under the Convention by exposing the applicant to inhuman living conditions. Although the applicant had not even applied for asylum and had not adduced any evidence concerning his individual situation during his stay in Greece, the court argued that the applicant "should not be expected to bear the entire burden of proof."[33] In addition, the court concluded that the procedure for remedy under Greek law did not meet the requirements of Article 13 of the Convention that the competent body must be able to examine the substance of a complaint, and afford proper reparation.[34]

The *M.S.S.* decision attracted a considerable amount of attention not only because of the large number of pending cases before national courts in the Dublin states, but also because of its implications for the functioning of the Dublin system. The ECtHR's jurisprudence is limited to Member States' compliance with the ECHR rather than EU law. But its judgments have a legal and practical effect on the interpretation of EU law because the founding treaties of the European Union (primary law) as well as the various conventions and agreements in which Member States participate (secondary law) make reference to human rights guaranteed under the ECHR. The European Court of Justice therefore refers frequently to the ECtHR's jurisprudence on the human rights established by the ECHR. In addition, the Charter of Fundamental Rights, which, like treaty law, constitutes primary Union law, contains rights which are modeled according to the ECHR. However, outside the scope of human rights there is a clear distinction between EU law

---

31 *M.S.S. v. Belgium and Greece.*
32 Ibid., paragraphs 233, 234, 263, and 264.
33 Ibid., paragraph 352.
34 Ibid., paragraphs 387–97.

obligations (which are not within the ECtHR's jurisdiction) and Member States' obligations under the European Convention of Human Rights. It was therefore very surprising for the ECtHR to connect the content of Article 3 of the ECHR with secondary Union law in the *M.S.S.* decision.

The court described the general living conditions of asylum seekers in Greece at length. While acknowledging that Article 3 of the ECHR cannot be interpreted as obliging the high contracting parties to provide everyone with a home or a certain standard of living,[35] the court decided that this particular case "cannot be considered in those terms."[36] It distinguished its judgment from previous, more restrictive, rulings with the argument that the obligation to provide accommodation and material conditions "has now entered into positive law and the Greek authorities are bound to comply with their own legislation, which transposes community law, namely directive 2003/9 laying down minimum standards for the reception of asylum seekers in the Member States."[37] The court also pointed "to the applicant's status as an asylum seeker and, as such, a member of a particularly underprivileged and vulnerable population group in need of special protection."[38] The court therefore came to the conclusion that the applicant was in a "situation of extreme material poverty."

2. The *N.S.* Judgment

Shortly after the *M.S.S.* decision, the European Court of Justice was called upon to decide a very similar case, this time of Afghan asylum seekers who had arrived in the United Kingdom after entering the European Union through Greece.[39] The ECJ has jurisdiction over EU law, including EU Fundamental Rights and in particular Article 4 of the Charter of Fundamental Rights (Prohibition of Inhuman Treatment and Torture). The court's proceedings received even more attention than those of the ECtHR, because the rules on the application of the Dublin system would be considered binding Union law for all Member States. They could even have implications for the European legislature if the court made a pronouncement on the meaning of the EU Charter of Fundamental Rights.

The first question the court considered was whether the issue of admitting an asylum seeker under the "sovereignty clause" of the Dublin Regulation, in derogation from its general rules, was within the scope of application of Union law. There was no question that the interpretation of the Dublin Regulation was within the jurisprudence of the court; it was, however, doubtful whether in the case under ques-

---

35 See *Müslim v. Turkey*, Applicant No. 53566/99 (European Court of Human Rights, 2005), paragraph 85.
36 Ibid., paragraph 250.
37 Ibid.
38 *Aorsus and others vs. Croatia*, Applicant No. 15766/03 (European Court of Human Rights, 2010), http://hudoc.echr.coe.int/sites/eng/pages/search.aspx?i=001-97689#.
39 *N.S. v Secretary of State for the Home Department.*

tion the fundamental rights laid down in the Charter on Fundamental Rights were applicable. A lively debate during the Lisbon Negotiations concluded with the decision that Charter provisions are applicable for Member States only in applying Union law.[40] Opinion among participating Member States was split, with some arguing that a decision under Article 2 (2) of the Dublin Regulation did not concern Union law since it was within the discretion of the Member States to make use of that clause. The court dismissed this argument since the discretionary power granted under the Dublin Regulation was to be considered as "an integral part" of Common European Asylum System provided for by the EU Treaty and developed by the EU legislature.[41]

Like the ECtHR, the ECJ arrived at the conclusion that European Union law precludes the application of a "rebuttable presumption" that the responsible Member State under the Dublin Regulation observes the fundamental rights of the European Union. But the reasons provided in the judgment were substantially different in the European Court of Justice's perspective.

In contrast to the ECtHR, the ECJ devoted substantial effort to defining the precarious border between the individual rights of asylum seekers to a fair asylum procedure and the public interest in a functioning European asylum system. The court stressed the principle of mutual confidence on which the Dublin Regulation is based and emphasized its importance for rationalizing the treatment of asylum claims, avoiding blockages in the system caused by multiple (or successive) claims by the same applicant, and preventing forum-shopping.

The court acknowledged that the principal objective of the Dublin Regulation to speed up the handling of claims could only be achieved if the treatment of asylum seekers in all Member States complied with the requirements of the Charter, the Geneva Convention and the European Convention on Human Rights. On the basis of this assumption the court proceeded to examine individual risks of violations of fundamental rights in the case of major operational problems in a given Member State. It concluded that neither "any infringement of a fundamental right by the Member State responsible" nor any infringement of EU directives (on the reception of asylum seekers, recognition as refugee, or asylum procedures) would affect the functioning of the Dublin system and prevent the transfer of an asylum seeker to the responsible Member State.[42] In the words of the court, what is at stake,

> "is the raison d'être of the European Union and the creation of an area of freedom, security and justice and, in particular, the

---

[40] Article 51 (1) of the European Convention on Human Rights. For the legislative history, see Peter J. Tettinger and Klaus Stern, eds. Kölner Gemeinschaftskommentar zur *Europäische Grundrechte-Charta* (Munich: CH Beck, 2006).
[41] *N.S. v Secretary of State for the Home Department,* Judgment at no. 65.
[42] *N.S. v Secretary of State for the Home Department,* Judgment paragraphs 82, 84.

common European asylum system, based on mutual confidence and a presumption of compliance, by other Member States, with European Union law and in particular fundamental rights."[43]

As reasons for refuting the assumption of safety, the court identified "systemic deficiencies in the asylum procedure and in the reception conditions of asylum seekers," which amount to substantial grounds for believing that the asylum seeker would face a real risk of being subjected to inhuman or degrading treatment.

With regard to the evidence an asylum seeker must produce in support of a claim, the ECJ seemed to follow the argument of the ECtHR on the relevance of general reports on the situation in the responsible Member State. Some governments had objected that the applicant did not provide sufficient evidence to establish an individual risk. The ECJ argued that as the reports were relevant and must have been known to the Member States ordering the transfer, reports of nongovernmental and governmental organizations were sufficient to establish systemic deficiencies. However, the court left other questions outstanding — in particular the question of effective legal protection. Some governments had argued that in spite of general deficiencies, the Greek system made adequate appeal procedures available to transferred asylum seekers. The ECtHR in the *M.S.S.* case, in contrast, had found that Greek law violated Article 13 of the European Convention on Human Rights as it allowed a request for a stay of execution only exceptionally, under an "extremely urgent procedure."[44] According to that court, Greek law did not provide such possibilities since there was insufficient examination of the merits of the alleged risk of a violation.[45]

The ECJ made no pronouncement on the question of whether judicial protection requires the suspension of all rights of appeal. According to Article 19 (2) of the Dublin Regulation, a decision not to examine the application and to transfer the applicant to the responsible Member State may be subject to an appeal or a review. Appeal or review shall not, however, suspend the implementation of the transfer unless the courts or competent bodies so decide, on a case-by-case basis, if national legislation allows for this. It is by no means clear whether states — in making use of their competence to regulate their judicial procedures — are subject to Article 47 of the Charter of Fundamental Rights. Even if the ECJ applies the principle of effective judicial remedy (Article 47) to the national rules on interim judicial protection, it remains to be seen whether effectual judicial protection requires the suspension of an appeal until a court decision has been made, either in the interim judicial protection procedure or in the procedure on the substance of the claim.

---

43 *N.S. v Secretary of State for the Home Department,* Judgment paragraph 83.
44 In the court's view, Article 13 requires the competent body to be able to examine the substance of the complaint and effect proper reparation.
45 *M.S.S. v. Belgium and Greece,* Paragraph 389.

In its proposal for a recast of the Dublin Regulation,[46] the European Commission suggested that in the event of an appeal or review concerning a transfer decision, the authority in question must decide within seven working days whether or not the person concerned may remain in the territory of the Member State concerned, and that no transfer shall take place before the decision is taken.[47]

C. Application of the Nonrefoulement Principle Outside the European Union

Following the pronouncement on the *M.S.S.* case, the European Court of Human Rights passed a judgment on another highly sensitive issue concerning the control of external borders according to the Schengen and Frontex rules. In the *Hirsi Jamaa* judgment,[48] the court found that Italy's agreements with Libya on the return of migrants intercepted off the coast of Italy were incompatible with Italy's obligations under the European Convention of Human Rights. Italy has been heavily criticized by human-rights organizations, UNHCR, and the European Commission, who have argued that Libya cannot be considered a safe third country. It was therefore unsurprising that ECtHR found Libya to be an unsuitable place for return of a person looking for protection.

The court's reasoning on the obligations of Member States to afford protection outside their own borders, and in particular at sea, has far-reaching consequences for the EU asylum system. The judgment raises a number of questions that will challenge the EU's efforts to use Frontex to control its external borders. The court stated that "whenever the State through its agents operating outside its territory exercises control and authority over an individual, and thus jurisdiction, the State is under an obligation under Article 1 [ECHR] to secure to that individual the rights and freedoms under Section 1 of the Convention that are relevant to the situation of that individual."[49] This ruling implies that Member States are responsible for attending to the rights of unauthorized migrants who are detected or apprehended by Frontex, but leaves unresolved the controversial issue of which Member State is responsible in any particular situation.

This does not necessarily mean that all obligations arising from EU secondary law and concerning claims of international protection are immediately applicable to the treatment of unauthorized migrants or applicants for asylum, since the ECtHR deals only with refoulement

---

46 See Hermann, "Commentary."
47 Council of the European Union, "Council Document 17831/11 Amended proposal for a Directive of the European Parliament and of the Council on common procedures for granting and withdrawing international protection status," December 13, 2011), accessed from Statewatch, www.statewatch.org/news/2011/dec/eu-council-asylum-procedures-17831-11.pdf.
48 *Hirsi Jamaa and others v. Italy.*
49 Ibid., Paragraph 74.

under Article 3 of the ECHR rather than broader EU obligations. Nevertheless, the judgment is in striking contrast to the judgments of the US Supreme Court[50] and the High Court of Australia,[51] as it extends the duty of admission and examination of claims for international protection to any situation in which a governmental body exercises control outside a state's territory. The court concluded that the applicants had "no access to a procedure to identify them and to assess their personal circumstances before they were returned to Libya" and observed that on the Italian military ships "there were neither interpreters nor legal advisers among the personnel on board."[52]

There are considerable challenges to applying this judgment. It is difficult to see how Italian coast guard or Frontex ships could be equipped to organize procedures and provide legal advice at sea. The court judgment may therefore amount to an obligation to take irregular migrants to the European Union and allow them a regular procedure. Since this would be difficult for states participating in Frontex operations to accept or manage, it further highlights the need to develop a distribution mechanism within the European Union. It also creates a disincentive for migrants to use flight routes, where there is a high chance of being picked up by an EU Member State or an EU agency.

A recent proposal by the Asylum Working Party of the Council of the European Union directly mentions the question of ensuring that migrants have access to a fair examination procedure.[53] In regard to persons carrying out surveillance of land and maritime borders or conducting border checks, it states that "where those persons are present in the territorial waters of a Member State they should be disembarked on land and then have their applications examined in accordance with this Directive."[54]

V. Conclusions and Recommendations

The Dublin system will remain a cornerstone of the Common European Asylum System. The ECJ's judgment in the *N.S.* case has in principle confirmed the functioning of the Dublin system by ensuring that it is only suspended in cases of systemic failures. Attempts to suspend its operation based upon individual examinations of safety — as the court

---

50 *Sale v. Haitian Centers Council*, 509 US 155(US Supreme Court, 1993), www.law.cornell.edu/supct/html/92-344.ZO.html.
51 *Minister for Immigration and Multicultural Affairs v. Haji Ibrahim*, 55 S 157/1999 (High Court of Australia, 2000), paragraph 136, www.refworld.org/cgi-bin/texis/vtx/rwmain?page=category&category=LEGAL&publisher=&type=CASELAW&coi=SOM&docid=3ae6b7600&skip=0.
52 Ibid., Paragraph 202.
53 Council of the European Union, "Council Document 17831/11 Amended proposal for a Directive of the European Parliament and of the Council on common procedures for granting and withdrawing international protection status."
54 Ibid., Recital no. 21.

rightly noted — would be equivalent to a collapse of the system. Therefore, the European legislature, in amending the Dublin Regulation, can expect the court to promote the project of a common European asylum system based on mutual trust.

The problem of burden-sharing, however, has not yet been solved. The ECJ explicitly refers to Greece's challenges resulting from a disproportionate burden of refugees. The Commission has submitted a proposal to suspend the application of the Dublin Regulation and amend it in order to mitigate the criterion of first entry. The European Commission's authorization to suspend the responsibility criteria may have very unwanted effects, however. At present, transfers to Greece are practically suspended by all EU Member States on the basis of national decisions under the Dublin Regulation. This may, in effect, increase migrant inflows by encouraging more migrants to reach their desired EU destination via Greece. Suspension authorizations can therefore hardly be considered a remedy to the problem of a mass influx at the external borders of the Schengen States.

The original expectation was that a strict system of exclusive responsibility would discourage migrants from using the asylum procedure as a means to an otherwise unobtainable residence permit. The appeal of lodging an asylum application depends on reaching the desired country of destination within the European Union and being able to remain there for a substantial amount of time. In spite of the adoption of the return directive and efforts to speed up the asylum procedure, the existing administrative and judicial procedures do result in a degree of humanitarian protection or regular residence in a large majority of cases.

The Dublin system of exclusive responsibility and the project to harmonize European legislation with the aim of speeding up the asylum procedure is only a part of the problem. Control of illegal immigration can only be achieved if illegal entry and residence is no longer perceived as attractive on the basis of a cost/benefit analysis compared with the expenses for organized smuggling. This aim can only be achieved if recourse to additional administrative or judicial procedures is restricted and effective European return procedures are put in place once a claim for international protection has been rejected. One possibility for the future may be the Europeanization of asylum procedures with strict time limitations and a European return management system, which in turn require considerable cooperation with sending countries. Whatever the path forward, the stakes are high: the capacity of nation-states to control irregular migration, either directly or through EU cooperation, is basic to border security.

Works Cited

Aorsus and others vs. Croatia. 2010. Applicant No. 15766/03, European Court of Human Rights. http://hudoc.echr.coe.int/sites/eng/pages/search.aspx?i=001-97689#.

Bank, Roland. 2009. Das Elgafaji-Urteil des EuGH und seine Bedeutung für den Schutz von Personen, die vor bewaffneten Konflikten fliehen. *Neue Zeitschrift für Verwaltungsrecht* 11: 695-99.

Bitoulas, Alexandros. 2013. Asylum applicants and first instance decisions on asylum applications. Eurostat, Data in Focus, May 2013. Brussels: European Union. http://epp.eurostat.ec.europa.eu/cache/ITY_OFFPUB/KS-QA-13-005/EN/KS-QA-13-005-EN.PDF.

Canadian Council for Refugees v. Canada. 2007. F C 1262, Canadian Federal Court. www.refworld.org/docid/474fe8d62.html.

Carrera, Sergio, Elspeth Guild, Massimo Merlino, and Joanna Parkin. 2011. *A Race Against Solidarity: The Schengen-Regime and the Franco-Italian Affair.* Brussels: Centre for European Policy Study. www.ceps.be/book/race-against-solidarity-schengen-regime-and-franco-italian-affair.

Council of the European Union. 2001. Directive 2001/55/EC on minimum standards for giving temporary protection in the event of a mass influx of displaced persons and on measures promoting a balance of efforts between Member States in receiving such persons and bearing the consequences thereof. July 20, 2001, EUR-Lex L 212. http://eur-lex.europa.eu/LexUriServ/LexUriServ.do?uri=CELEX:32001L0055:EN:HTML.

_____. 2003. Council Directive 2003/9/EC laying down minimum standards for the reception of asylum seekers. January 27, 2003, EUR-Lex L 31/18. Last amended by L 304, November 14, 2008. http://eur-lex.europa.eu/LexUriServ/LexUriServ.do?uri=OJ:L:2003:031:0018:0025:EN:PDF.

_____. 2003. Council Regulation (EC) No 343/2003 establishing the criteria and mechanisms for determining the Member State responsible for examining an asylum application lodged in one of the Member States by a third-country national. February 18, 2003, EUR-Lex L 050. http://eur-lex.europa.eu/LexUriServ/LexUriServ.do?uri=CELEX:32003R0343:EN:HTML.

_____. 2004. Council Directive 2004/83/EC on minimum standards for the qualification and status of third-country nationals or stateless persons as refugees or as persons who otherwise need international protection and the content of the protection granted. April 29, 2004, EUR-Lex L 304. http://eur-lex.europa.eu/LexUriServ/LexUriServ.do?uri=CELEX:32004L0083:EN:HTML.

_____. 2004. Council Regulation (EC) No. 2007/2004 establishing a European Agency for the Management of Operational Cooperation at the External Borders of the Member States of the European Union. http://europa.eu/legislation_summaries/justice_freedom_security/free_movement_of_persons_asylum_immigration/l33216_en.htm.

_____. 2005. Council Directive 2005/85/EC on minimum standards on procedures in Member States for granting and withdrawing refugee status. December 1, 2005, EUR-Lex L 326/13. http://eur-lex.europa.eu/LexUriServ/LexUriServ.do?uri=OJ:L:2005:326:0013:0034:EN:PDF.

———. 2011. Council Document 17831/11, Amended proposal for a Directive of the European Parliament and of the Council on common procedures for granting and withdrawing international protection status. December 13, 2011. Accessed from Statewatch, www.statewatch.org/news/2011/dec/eu-council-asylum-procedures-17831-11.pdf.

European Parliament and Council of the European Union. 2006. Regulation (EC) No 562/2006 establishing a Community Code on the rules governing the movement of persons across borders (Schengen Borders Code). March 15, 2006, EUR-Lex L 105/1. http://eur-lex.europa.eu/LexUriServ/LexUriServ.do?uri=OJ:L:2006:105:0001:0032:EN:PDF.

———. 2011. Directive 2011/95 EU on standards for the qualification of third-country nationals or stateless persons as beneficiaries of international protection, for a uniform status for refugees or for persons eligible for subsidiary protection, and for the content of the protection granted. December 13, 2011, EUR-Lex L 337/9. http://eur-lex.europa.eu/LexUriServ/LexUriServ.do?uri=OJ:L:2011:337:0009:0026:EN:PDF.

European Union. 2007. Treaty of Lisbon Amending the Treaty on European Union and the Treaty Establishing the European Community. 2007/C 306/01, December 13, 2007, Article 78 TFEU.

Federal Administrative Court (Germany). 2005. FAC of 29.05.2008, case no. 10 C 11/07, May 29, 2005, BVerwGE 131, 186, para. 30 ff. Accessed from European Database of Asylum Law, www.asylumlawdatabase.eu/en/case-law/germany-%E2%80%93-federal-administrative-court-29-may-2008-10-c-1107#content.

Hailbronner, Kay. 2010. Asylum Law. In *EU Immigration and Asylum Law*, ed. Kay Hailbronner. Oxford: Hart Publishing.

Hailbronner, Kay and Daniel Thym. 2011. Vertrauen im Europäischen Asylsystem. *Neue Zeitschrift für Verwaltungsrecht* 4 (21).

Hermann, Matthias. 2010. Commentary. In *EU Immigration and Asylum Law*, ed. Kay Hailbronner. Oxford: Hart Publishing.

Hirsi Jamaa and others v. Italy. 2012. 27765/09, European Court of Human Rights. http://hudoc.echr.coe.int/sites/eng/pages/search.aspx?i=001-109231#.

Kasimis, Charalambos. 2012. Greece: Illegal Immigration in the Midst of a Crisis. *Migration Information Source*, March 2012. www.migrationinformation.org/Profiles/display.cfm?ID=884.

K.R.S. v. United Kingdom. 2008. Applicant No. 32733/08, European Court of Human Rights. http://hudoc.echr.coe.int/sites/eng/pages/search.aspx?i=001-90500#.

Meki Elgafaji and Noor Elgafaji v. Staatssecretaris van Justitie. 2009. C-465/07 ECR I-921, European Court of Justice. http://curia.europa.eu/juris/celex.jsf?celex=62007CJ0465&lang1=en&type=NOT&ancre=.

Minister for Immigration and Multicultural Affairs v. Haji Ibrahim. 2000. 55 S 157/1999, High Court of Australia. www.refworld.org/cgi-bin/texis/vtx/rwmain?page=category&category=LEGAL&publisher=&type=CASELAW&coi=SOM&docid=3ae6b7600&skip=0.

M.S.S. v. Belgium and Greece. 2011. Applicant No. 30696/09, European Court of Justice. http://ec.europa.eu/anti-trafficking/entity.action;jsessionid=hD6vRTj DbDsK7qnvQZt8Tjy4hGMWvKqLP6WhTjM0gc0TJKXSr1Md!1062222535?p ath=Legislation+and+Case+Law/Case+Law/CASE+OF+M.S.S.+v.+BELGIUM+ AND+GREECE.

Müslim v. Turkey. 2005. Applicant No. 53566/99, European Court of Human Rights. http://echr.ketse.com/doc/53566.99-en-20050426/.

N.S. v. Secretary of State for the Home Department. 2011. Case C-411/10, European Court of Human Rights. http://eur-lex.europa.eu/LexUriServ/LexUriServ.do?uri=CELEX:62010CJ0411:EN:HTML.

Peek, Marcus. 2010. Commentary. In *EU Immigration and Asylum Law*, ed. Kay Hailbronner. Oxford: Hart Publishing.

Peers, Steve. 2011. *EU Justice and Home Affairs Law*, 3rd edition. Oxford: Oxford University Press.

Regina v. Secretary of State for the Home Department Ex Parte Jogathas. 2002. UCHL 36, House of Lords. www.publications.parliament.uk/pa/ld199899/ldjudgmt/jd990708/obrien01.htm.

Sale v. Haitian Centers Council. 1993. 509 US 155, US Supreme Court. www.law.cornell.edu/supct/html/92-344.ZO.html.

Skordas, Achilles. 2010. Commentary. In *EU Immigration and Asylum Law*, ed. Kay Hailbronner. Oxford: Hart Publishing.

Tettinger, Peter J. and Klaus Stern, eds. 2006. *Kölner Gemeinschaftskommentar zur Europäische Grundrechte-Charta.* Munich: CH Beck.

Thielemann, Eiko R. 2003. Between Interests and Norms: Explaining Burden-Sharing in the European Union. *Journal of Refugee Studies* 16 (3): 253–73.

Thym, Daniel. 2011. *Menschenrechtliche Feinjustierung des Dublinsystems zur Asylzuständigkeitsabgrenzung — zu den Folgewirkungen des Straßburger M.S.S. — Urteils.* Baden-Baden: Zeitschrift für Ausländerrecht und Ausländerpolitik.

United Nations High Commissioner for Refugees (UNHCR). 1994. *The Principle of Non-Refoulement as a Norm of Customary International Law. Response to the Questions Posed to UNHCR by the Federal Constitutional Court of the Federal Republic of Germany in Cases 2 BvR 1938/93, 2 BvR 1953/93, 2 BvR 1954/93.* January 31, 1994. www.refworld.org/docid/437b6db64.html.

CHAPTER 3

BORDER INSECURITY IN CENTRAL AMERICA'S NORTHERN TRIANGLE

Ralph Espach
Center for Naval Analyses

Daniel Haering
Francisco Marroquín University

I. Introduction: Neglected Borders, from the Colonial Era to the Present[1]

Several factors contribute to a historical pattern of government neglect of peripheral territories in Central America. Colonialism left behind highly concentrated economic and political systems: countries run by and principally for their wealthiest families, who tended to live in the capitals and pay little heed to events outside the key economic centers. Severe racial discrimination has also contributed to the historic neglect of border regions where indigenes, Afro-Caribbeans, mestizos, and Creoles compose a relatively large share of the local population.[2]

These hinterlands and porous borders, generally neglected, have periodically provided areas where outside powers or inside insurgencies could operate. Though a century apart, the British merchants and navy

---

1 The authors would like to express their appreciation to the many officials of the Guatemalan government and the Democratic Security Program of the System for Central American Integration (SICA) who shared their time and understanding of these issues, especially Werner Ovalle, who directs the Border Security Program. The authors also thank their friend and colleague Javier Q. Meléndez for leading them to the issue — complex, both conceptually and operationally — of border security. This chapter first appeared as a report for the October 2011 meeting of the Regional Migration Study Group convened by the Migration Policy Institute (MPI) and the Latin American Program of the Woodrow Wilson Center.
2 Javier Q. Meléndez, Roberto B. Orozco, Sergio M. Moya, and Miguel R. López, *Una Aproximación a la Problemática de la Criminalidad Organizada en las Comunidades del Caribe y de Fronteras* (Managua, Nicaragua: Instituto de Estudios Estratégicos y Políticas Públicas, 2010): 14-6.

of the 19th century and the US and Cuban special forces of the Cold War era both exploited the region's porous borders and ungoverned territories to conduct their operations.

The latest actors to take advantage of the region's uncontrolled borders are Mexican-based trafficking cartels.[3] Drug traffickers have operated in Central America since at least the 1980s, but increased anti-drug operations in the Caribbean region beginning in the 1990s led Colombian cartels to favor overland routes through Central America and Mexico to cross the Mexico-US border.[4] The Colombians moved products through the region largely by buying the services of local trafficking networks. Over time, those networks grew into competitive cartels themselves in Mexico, where crossing into the United States was highly profitable. In the early 2000s, Mexico's trafficking industry began to concentrate, becoming more conflictive and violent. The leading cartels also expanded their operations from merely trafficking the products of others to the buying of products upstream, in Colombia or elsewhere, overseeing production, and controlling transit region wide. As they did so, their profits skyrocketed.

These Mexican cartels began to operate in Central America, particularly in Guatemala, chiefly by buying the services of local trafficking networks. These relatively peaceful arrangements began to break down in 2008, due to Guatemalan thievery or *tumbes*, which led to high-profile mass killings where Mexican cartels and the paramilitary Zetas group first showed their presence in Guatemala. Since then, the Mexican cartels and their local partners have sought increasingly to control routes themselves. Many of these routes lie along the Guatemalan coast, as drugs are brought in by boat and then transferred onto land for transit into Mexico. Other routes come in from Honduras, with the drugs being flown in from Venezuela or brought in via boat. Over the past 18 months, evidence indicates that the Sinaloa and the Zetas drug cartels have increased their presence in Guatemala and Honduras, and conduct a wider range of their operations there — recruiting, training, and drug processing — than they used to. They also sell more of their product locally, which fuels local gang activity and urban violence.

---

3   Mexican cartels including the Sinaloa Group, los Zetas, and the Gulf Cartel are best known for the trafficking of narcotics. However, they are known to be involved to varying degrees in many other types of trafficking as well, including the trafficking of weapons, humans, and precursor chemicals (for manufacturing narcotics).
4   For a good account on the evolution of drug trafficking in the region see Julie López, "Guatemala´s Crossroads: Democratization of Violence and Second Chances" (Working Paper Series on Organized Crime in Central America, Woodrow Wilson International Center for Scholars, Washington, DC, December 2010): 4-29, www.wilsoncenter.org/sites/default/files/Lopez.Guatemala.pdf; and Ralph Espach, Javier Melendez, Daniel Haering, and Miguel Castillo, *Criminal Organizations and Illicit Trafficking in Guatemala's Border Communities* (Washington, DC: Center for Naval Analyses, 2011): 9-19, www.cna.org/research/2011/criminal-organizations-illicit-trafficking.

II. Border Insecurity in Central America's Northern Triangle

The borders between Guatemala and Mexico, El Salvador, and Honduras are porous and uncontrolled across most of their length. There are police and customs agents at most points where major highways cross the border, main ports, and commercial airports, but outside these locations and away from urban areas borders are mostly unmonitored by state forces. Hundreds of miles of borders, through mountains and jungles and along rivers, are unmarked. In 2011 Guatemalan officials estimated that, along that country's borders, there were nearly 125 unmonitored "blind crossings" sufficiently wide and maintained to allow the passage of small trucks.[5]

Figure 1. Formal Border Crossings among Mexico, Guatemala, El Salvador, and Honduras

Source: Center for Naval Analyses (CNA), based on data from the Red de Seguridad y Defensa de America Latina (RESDAL), *Indice de Seguridad Publica y Ciudadana en America Latina* (Buenos Aires, Argentina: RESDAL, 2011).

---

5 Marizza Alejandra Herrera, *Retos y principios para el combate del crimen transnacional en regiones fronterizas: El caso de la frontera Guatemala-México* (Santiago de Chile: Centro de Estudios Estratégicos, 2011): 12.

Many of the official crossing points, where they exist, are primitive and lax in their standards, without reliable access to electricity or phone service, without bathrooms, and with unarmed agents.[6] Along the Guatemala-Mexico border there are eight official crossing points, but only four of those are consistently open and manned.[7] In addition, illegal airstrips available for the unloading of drugs number in the hundreds. Mexico's President, Enrique Peña Nieto, has indicated his administration will seek to modernize the checkpoints and create a border patrol along the Mexico-Guatemala border in hopes of facilitating legal traffic and reducing unlawful entries.

The current level of border insecurity exists within the context of small, poorly trained, and under-resourced public security forces in general. Security and defense institutions and policies have been largely ignored, especially in El Salvador and Guatemala, since the end of the brutal civil wars of the 1980s. These countries' peace processes included agreements between the governments and opposition forces to reduce the size and resources of the armed forces, to eliminate existing national intelligence institutions, and to replace them with strong public security forces. Militaries were cut dramatically, but unfortunately the process of police rebuilding and reform became politicized and slow due to budgetary cuts, and has only been partly completed.

Attitudes toward the military and security in general are sharply polarized even today, between former guerrillas and their sympathizers and those who advocate for strong national forces. Elected governments have often vacillated from one side to the other, spurring inconsistency and undermining any progress achieved by predecessors. The Honduran policy community is not polarized in the same way, but its police and armed forces have suffered like those of El Salvador and Guatemala from extremely limited budgets and politicians who are generally uninterested in security issues.

Security and defense policies in the countries of northern Central America, including policies and programs for border security, share a common set of problems:

- *Insufficient funds.* Central American countries spend relatively little money on their public security forces, both police and military.[8] This is due to their weak tax regimes (inefficient collection and tax evasion are common problems) and their

---

6 Interview with Werner Ovalle, Director of programs and border security for the SICA Border Security Program, January 2012. On file with authors.
7 Herrera, *Retos y principios para el combate del crimen transnacional en regiones fronterizas.*
8 In 2011 Guatemala spent around $580 million on total defense (combining military and Ministry of Governance budgets), El Salvador $439 million, and Honduras $335 million — levels significantly higher than just a few years back. Their combined spending is under $1.5 billion a year, compared against estimates of the profits from drug trafficking at around $10 billion-$15 billion, which does not include money made from smuggling weapons, humans, and other contraband.

civilian governments' long-standing lack of interest in national security issues. Also, within the range of security issues, governments tend to view border security as a lower priority than citizen security in urban areas, where most crime occurs.

- **Weak institutions and mismatched competencies.** These governments feature ill-defined civil-military controls;[9] poorly trained, equipped, and paid police forces; understaffed and underfunded customs and migration-control agencies; and unreliable judiciary institutions. Unable to effectively coordinate their own interagency efforts on security, their problems are compounded at the bilateral and multilateral levels when different agencies must coordinate across borders. In addition, government and agency structures and authorities often differ from country to country, further complicating efforts at effective collaboration.

- **Lack of continuity.** Without coherent and strong government institutions, especially functional agencies and a legislature, political will to take on complex issues dissipates rapidly. In these countries, national plans, programs, and initiatives tend to have life spans of only a couple of years and almost never survive executive turnovers, which are made mandatory by constitutional single-term limits.[10] This lack of continuity severely undermines the effectiveness and legitimacy of ambitious government reform and policy projects.

- **Corruption.** The problem of corruption — rampant across the region — further complicates and weakens these governments' security efforts. Even when policies are well designed and implemented, have broad support, and involve new technologies, systems, and infrastructure to improve state performance, their effectiveness is not guaranteed due to corruption. This has proven true regarding border security measures, where new technologies, training, infrastructure, and other resources do little to counteract local practices of bribing and threatening harm to law and customs enforcement officers.

---

9 These countries' national constitutions give the armed forces broad authority, including the protection of national order in times of political crisis. Such authority blurs the lines of command and control, sustains a political role for military leadership, and complicates civilian-military coordination even in basic operations and functions such as intelligence management and military-police joint operations.

10 El Salvador, where re-election is permitted, is the exception. This helps to account for the relatively stable political system in that country.

III. The Socioeconomic Dynamics of Border Communities

Border communities in the region tend to be cut off from most national services and systems due to poor transportation and communications infrastructures. Residents tend to focus on events, people, opportunities, and politics in the local region — including just across the border — more so than those at the national level.[11] For many residents of border communities, those national borders are not porous — they are nonexistent. People will cross the border a few times a day to work; to visit families or friends; or to buy or sell grains, flour, livestock, or gasoline at a better price. The economic character of these communities rests on this activity, and in some cases (e.g., when services such as medical care or electricity can be accessed only across the border) depend on it for their survival. In many cases the economies of border communities are more closely linked to markets and supplies on the other side of the border than they are to those within the same country.

Local security is tenuous at best. In most border communities away from major highway crossing points, the formal rule of law does not exist. National police forces have minimal, if any, presence. In communities where police are present, jails and courts are often several hours away by road, limiting the effectiveness of police activity. Especially in Guatemala, vigilante justice is common.

These countries' public security budgets do not afford a police presence in small communities. In El Salvador, there is one police officer for every 294 citizens. The ratio in Guatemala is 1 to 651 and in Honduras 1 to 715,[12] compared to 1 to 223 in the United States. Central American police tend to be concentrated in urban areas where they are easier to support. In smaller border communities where there are police units, these consist of just two to four officers and typically lack working vehicles, fuel, and reliable communication systems. Because most police officers are recruited in the main cities, they tend to be of different ethnicity from the local residents and are often unable to speak the local languages (in indigenous communities). According to interviews and anecdotal information, the police in these communities often feel distrusted by the local population, lack basic understanding about the community and the criminal elements and conflicts within it, and feel outnumbered and outgunned. In some cases they choose not to patrol far from their station or the main streets, and do not venture outside

---

11 The same is true for rural communities near borders in the United States and many other countries. What is striking about the Central American case, however, is that these are small countries and these border communities are not, in fact, so distant from the capitals and main urban centers. Their isolation reflects the low quality of these nations' transportation and communications infrastructures.

12 Marcela Donadio, *Índice de Seguridad Pública y Ciudadana en América Latina. El Salvador, Guatemala y Honduras* (Buenos Aires, Argentina: RESDAL, 2011): 9, www.resdal.org/libro-seg/.

the town even when there are reports of criminal activity, because it is too dangerous.[13]

In many border communities, the lack of any state presence means that local nonstate groups assume the government's role as provider of key services, including security. Among groups that may provide public services are tribal authorities, informal groups of leading families, and religious organizations. In terms of security, informal, local self-defense institutions are not uncommon in isolated communities, either existing permanently or forming as ad hoc responses to a perceived threat (vigilantism). In many border areas, especially near smuggling routes, local criminal organizations (which often overlap with, or include, these other more traditional centers of authority) play this role.[14] In many cases these "parallel government" structures involve local landowners, business owners, nongovernmental organization (NGO) operators, and politicians, with varying degrees of awareness of and involvement in illicit trafficking. For example, the same network will arrange on one day the delivery of medicines for the community's public clinic or books for the school, and the next the killing of individuals believed to be extorting local businesses.[15]

Relations between border community residents, community organizations, political structures, and organized-criminal groups are often complex, with long historical precedents. As is well documented, criminal groups often rely upon the existence of a government that is functional enough to provide basic services such as public order and working infrastructure, but not strong enough to interfere with their criminal operations. Organized-criminal groups often threaten and/or bribe local political leaders and police to leave them alone — a task made easier by the fact that in small communities most officials, politicians, and landowners know one other's families. In some cases, these groups use their money and influence to penetrate or co-opt local political parties, mayors, and legislators. They frequently own land, farms, and local companies, and have ties to local NGOs, which allow them to bid for public projects and funds through which they can launder money and expand their wealth and political influence.[16]

Indeed, at least in Guatemala, evidence indicates that the surge in illicit trafficking since the early 2000s has helped these border communities' economies disproportionately as profits spill over into the

---

13 Interviews conducted by Ralph Espach and Center for Naval Analyses (CNA) colleagues with residents of border communities in Guatemala's San Marcos province (October 2010).
14 Espach et al., *Criminal Organizations and Illicit Trafficking*, 63-6. In the context of the long-standing absence of the rule of law, it is often difficult to distinguish local landowners and business owners, and their political and business partners, from criminal organizations because the same people are engaged in both legal and illegal activities.
15 Espach et al., *Criminal Organizations and Illicit Trafficking*, 45-54.
16 See Anonymous, *Grupos de poder en Petén: Territorio, política y negocios*; and Oscar Martínez, "La frontera de los Señores," *El Faro*, August 14, 2011, www.salanegra.elfaro.net/es/201108/cronicas/5018/.

local community. The border regions and key border towns have Guatemala's fastest-growing economies and populations. According to a recent study that examined the effects of illicit trafficking in three border communities in Guatemala, local residents of each community reported a readily observable increase in local consumption. In two cases families who lived outside of town near the border, and were most likely to be involved directly with border transit services, seemed to demonstrate especially fast-rising incomes.[17] School matriculation rates increased in these communities as well, attributed in part to the rising number of motorbikes and small vehicles owned by families in the countryside whose children used to be unable to attend school due to the distance from their homes.

Local residents and financial officers in these Guatemalan communities believe that much of their recent growth is the result of drug trafficking and money laundering; profits are evident in the newly expanded tomato fields, cattle ranches, gas stations, or palm plantations just out of town. Laundering money through such businesses is common because the heads of trafficking networks tend to be local citizens who run farms or other businesses in addition to their illicit activities. In regions where tax evasion is the norm, governments lack financial oversight and regulatory systems sophisticated enough to assess the extent of this activity.

IV. Types of Illicit Trafficking

In poorly serviced and poorly regulated regions such as these, illegal border crossings occur frequently and for numerous reasons. To the authors' knowledge, there are no available data on border crossings — legal and registered or otherwise — only estimates. According to recent research, reporting, and interviews with officials and residents in border communities, by far the most frequent crossings are by local residents who cross to buy or sell legal goods for personal use, access services, or visit family or friends. This activity is typical of border life and, in some cases, essential for local well-being. While not in itself illegal, these crossings are made in part to get around price controls and other regulations or taxes, and therefore in aggregate have some degree of negative economic impact on the local legal economy.[18] These types of border crossings, however, have few security implications.

---

17 Espach et al., *Criminal Organizations and Illicit Trafficking*, 41.
18 Though there are no reliable data on the volume of such activity and its impact, it is likely to be higher along the Guatemala-Mexico border than the other borders addressed in this chapter. The Guatemalan and Mexican economies are less integrated than those between Guatemala and El Salvador or Honduras, at least at the formal level, because Mexico is not a party to the 2006 Central America-4 (CA-4) Border Control Agreement that reduced border and customs restrictions for residents of El Salvador, Guatemala, Honduras, and Nicaragua.

Another relatively frequent activity is the ***smuggling of legal consumables for resale.*** This smuggling of goods such as gasoline, grains, vegetables, and packaged food is very common, especially in populated and heavily transited areas near the Guatemalan-Mexican border.[19] It is estimated to have a significant, negative impact on the legal national economy and producers. However, this activity tends to be widely dispersed, that is, carried out on a small scale by many individuals and families in a given community. As a result, compared to higher value and more logistically difficult forms of smuggling, this activity is not associated with violent crime.

Today, ***drug trafficking*** receives the most public attention because of the violent competition over smuggling routes among trafficking cartels such as the Sinaloa group and los Zetas,[20] and the enormous wealth drug profits generate.[21] Because of the volume of money involved, the relative ease of trafficking narcotics (as compared to humans or weapons), and the longevity of drug trafficking networks in the region (many of which date back at least to the 1980s), this activity seems to do more to distort local and national economies and to promote political corruption across the region than do other trafficking activities.[22] As routes are contended and law enforcement insufficient, drug trafficking also generates the highest rates of violence, though we must keep in mind that many of the same routes, networks, and organizations that traffic drugs also traffic — or oversee and profit from the trafficking of — humans and weapons and other goods.

Human smuggling takes many forms, most of them voluntary and involving the service of transit for a fee. As with drug trafficking, profitable human smuggling requires special services, logistics, and a network of service collaborators on both sides of the border. This activity tends to be concentrated among a few local service provid-

---

19   Again, the result of the lack of economic integration between these countries and numerous opportunities for border arbitrage and tariff evasion, related to policies such as Mexican price controls for gasoline.

20   There are two types of key players active today in drug trafficking through Guatemala: transnational Mexican cartels, which in recent years have operated directly in the region, and Central American *transportistas* that provide transport services to these and other larger foreign organizations. For a detailed explanation see Steven S. Dudley, *Drug Trafficking Organizations in Central America: Transportistas, Mexican Cartels and Maras* (Washington, DC: Woodrow Wilson International Center for Scholars, 2010), http://stevendudley.com/pdf/Wilson%20Center%20Central%20America%20Dudley%2005%2017%2010.pdf.

21   Estimates of the value and profits of the Central American drug trade differ widely. The 2010 *World Drug Report* from the UN Office of Drug Control (UNODC) estimates that the gross profit from regional trafficking is $4.6 billion, an amount comparable to the entire Guatemalan gross domestic product (GDP). See UNODC, *World Drug Report 2010* (New York: UNODC, 2010): 79, www.unodc.org/unodc/en/data-and-analysis/WDR-2010.html. The US government estimates the total value of the narcotics that are trafficked through the region at $40 billion to $60 billion.

22   See Anonymous, *Grupos de poder en Petén: Territorio, política y negocios;* also known as the Petén Report, it explains in great detail the corrupt networks that operate at a regional and national level and how these interact.

ers (e.g., *coyotes*, hotels, commercial transit companies), limiting the extent of public involvement. Criminal organizations are often involved, because they control access to those networks. In addition to voluntary smuggling, criminal organizations also traffic humans involuntarily for sexual exploitation or other reasons. Reliable estimates on the volume of human smuggling are hard to find, but anecdotally and according to the dramatic decline in arrests of illegal migrants made by US authorities on the US-Mexican border,[23] it is reasonable to conclude that human smuggling in the region has fallen significantly in recent years.

Weapons trafficking, particularly the trafficking of small firearms, is another serious problem on these borders. To our knowledge, there are no reliable estimates of the volume of weapons trafficked, nor the general direction of these flows. It is believed that many weapons are smuggled into Central America from Mexico, having been acquired originally in the United States. However, military-grade rifles, grenades, and other weapons seized in the region from organized-criminal groups, or used to commit crimes, often seem to come from local military supplies.[24]

Money laundering is an increasing problem in border communities across Central America, as traffickers invest a share of their profits in legal local enterprises including service companies, construction projects, gasoline stations, and agriculture.[25] According to a Guatemalan financial regulatory official, local traffickers and their partners tend to prefer to launder their money locally, where they know and understand the economic and political community well (and, presumably, can better monitor and interfere with potential regulatory efforts). Partly as a result of this local-level laundering, in recent years Guatemalan border cities have been the country's fastest-growing and most economically vibrant markets. Though often not viewed as a security issue, the distortionary effect this illegal money can have on local economies, and the additional penetration and influence the revenue provide organized-criminal groups, can further destabilize local communities.

The diversity of illicit activities associated with the exploitation of borders, and the fact that most have positive as well as negative conse-

---

23 The number of US arrests of illegal migrants at the border with Mexico totaled 327,577 in 2011, the lowest number since 1971. In comparison, in 2000 the United States arrested 1.64 million (see Nick Miroff and William Booth, "Arrests of Illegal Migrants on US-Mexico Border Plummet," *The Washington Post*, December 3, 2011), www.washingtonpost.com/world/americas/arrests-of-illegal-migrants-on-us-mexico-border-plummet/2011/12/02/gIQA6Op8PO_story.html.
24 Ronan Graham, "Honduras Guns Feeding Central America's Arms Trade," *Insightcrime.org*, August 12, 2011, www.insightcrime.org/news-analysis/honduras-guns-feeding-central-americas-arms-trade.
25 As with other illicit activities, the informality of the region's economies, especially at the rural level, makes it impossible to assess the scale of money laundering; interview with Susan Rojas, Director of IVE (the department of the Bank of Guatemala in charge of money laundering in the country). On file with authors.

quences for border residents and communities, underlies the complexity of border security policymaking.

V. Regional Border-Control Efforts and Challenges

In recent years, Central American governments have attempted to address border insecurity in various ways and at different levels: national, bilateral, and multilateral.

A. Border Security Policies and Programs at the National Level

Guatemala has not had a coherent border security strategy or policy for at least four years.[26] The government has ordered increases in police and military personnel sent to the border, without providing these forces any new resources. As a result, these border build-ups have been short-lived. In 2010 and 2011 the government reacted to a series of mass murders and confrontations with authorities by the Zetas cartel by imposing military rule in the border departments of Petén and Alta Verapaz. Though this calmed the areas for the weeks when the military was present, after their withdrawal reports indicate that these groups and their local partners reasserted control just as before. The new president, Otto Perez Molina, who took office in January 2012, released a national security plan in July 2012. In general terms it suffers from the same defects as previous policies: lack of specificity and absence of a comprehensive and thorough definition of the problem. As for the development of a border security strategy, it is clear that it still isn't a priority.

In February 2011 El Salvador announced a set of national security reforms focused on addressing deficiencies in the penal system, budgetary reforms, victims' services, and crime prevention. Within a year the army of 11,000 had added 6,300 new soldiers. Though border security was not one of the plan's five focus areas, it included policies to strengthen migration and customs controls, and sent an army battalion to patrol borders.[27] At the chapter's writing, the authors were unable to verify if these measures had been implemented, and to what effect.

Honduras, still shaken by the political crisis of 2009, in which the military played a central role, lacks a coherent national security program.

---

26 Guatemalan government officials interviewed by an investigator from the Ibn Khaldún International Research Center in Guatemala City in the fall of 2011 could not name a single border security policy, either current or in recent memory.
27 Sergio Arauz, "Cantidad de militares ha crecido un 57% en primer gobierno de izquierda," *El Faro*, December 7, 2011, http://elfaro.net/es/201112/noticias/6827/.

Nevertheless, in recent months the Honduran government has joined its neighbors in ordering military support for police operations in gang-infested areas, though not explicitly at the borders. News reports indicate that the area along the Honduras-Guatemala border is entirely controlled by trafficking groups with ties to the Mexican cartels, and that these groups effectively control local politics and the police.[28]

B. Border Security Policies and Programs at the Bilateral Level

At the bilateral level the region has seen some promising efforts at border control, particularly involving joint border patrols. For example, in December 2005 Guatemala and El Salvador formed a joint police unit that conducted combined patrols along the border. This joint unit operated for three years, but in 2009 was dissolved due to shifting priorities within the Guatemalan government and confusion over legal authorizations and procedures regarding arrests on foreign soil. In February 2012 Presidents Mauricio Funes of El Salvador and Otto Perez of Guatemala agreed to restate this binational police, and invited the government of Honduras to join those efforts.[29] Further details about the legal framework(s) and the *modus operandi* for these efforts, due to be in place by April 2012, were unavailable at the writing of this chapter.

Guatemala has also benefited from cooperation with Mexico, whose security forces are far larger and better equipped. In 2002 a Bilateral Guatemala-Mexico Commission formed a High-Level Border Security Group (GANSEF), an interagency group (including representatives from Belize) with the objective of improving information sharing and coordinating joint-security initiatives. In 2008 this group was reduced to only Mexico and Guatemala and its name was changed to the High-Level Mexico-Guatemala Security Group (GANSEG).[30] This group consists of the two nations' ministries of governance, supported by national strategic analysis agencies.[31] Though their titles are the same, in reality the ministries serve different functions in each country and are not equivalent, a problem that has kept GANSEG from functioning effectively.[32] GANSEG has also suffered from a lack of trust and agreement between

---

28 Martínez, "La frontera de los Señores."
29 Ovalle interview, January 23, 2012; see also EFE News Agency, "Guatemala y El Salvador integrarán Policía Binacional para fronteras," February 13, 2012, www.prensalibre.com/noticias/politica/Guatemala-Salvador-integraran-Policia-Binacional_0_645535659.html.
30 Herrera, *Retos y principios para el combate del crimen transnacional en regiones fronterizas: El caso de la frontera Guatemala-México.*
31 These are the Guatemalan Strategic Analysis Secretary (SAE) and Mexico's Center for Investigation and National Security (CISEN).
32 In Mexico the Ministry of Governance (Ministerio de Gobernación) is more focused on programs and strategies to democratize Mexican society by way of dialogue, consensus building, and ensuring order than it is on technical or operational matters of security, while the Guatemalan Ministry of Governance is completely focused on security.

the two national delegations, which has minimized the frequency of GANSEG meetings. For these reasons, underpinned by a general lack of political commitment on both sides, the GANSEF/GANSEG initiative has not proven an effective tool for dialogue or policy coordination.

The GANSEG case illustrates a problem common throughout the region, but especially challenging to the governments of Guatemala and Mexico: asymmetries between the countries' government institutions and/or structures. For example, in Mexico, state governments act with a great deal of autonomy. Mexican governors are publicly elected and have a wide range of responsibilities, including an important role in providing public security. In contrast, Guatemalan departmental governors are selected by the president and have few responsibilities and relatively little legitimacy in the eyes of citizens. They have no position within the chain of command of the national police or the armed forces. The result is that a Mexican governor who wants to speak with his or her counterpart in Guatemala does not call a departmental governor because that position cannot commit relevant state resources. The Mexican governor can choose to try to communicate with the national government, for example, the Ministry of Defense, but this requires adherence to diplomatic protocols and coordination with the Mexican national government, which complicates and slows the process.

Honduras has struggled to engage in bilateral border security agreements in the Northern Triangle region, with both Guatemala and El Salvador. Border relations between El Salvador and Honduras are complicated due to an international boundary dispute that goes back to colonial times. Although the International Court of Justice adjudicated the case in 1992, to this day the remote 347 kilometers are not clearly demarcated,[33] causing friction between the countries.

In the case of Honduran-Guatemalan border relations, a recent report by the Honduran Demarcation Commission states that the Honduran government has not had an effective state presence in its border zone for the past 75 years.[34] That evaluation reflects the challenges these regional neighbors face in building cross-border security coordination. The possibility of integrating Honduras in the project of combined patrols mentioned above with both El Salvador and Guatemala could be a good start.

---

[33] Mario Cerna, "Falta de fondos impide terminar la demarcación," *El Heraldo,* August 23, 2011, http://archivo.elheraldo.hn/Ediciones/2011/08/24/Noticias/Falta-de-fondos-impide-terminar-la-demarcacion/.
[34] See Mario Cerna, "Honduras sin presencia en la frontera con Guatemala desde hace 75 años," *El Heraldo*, August 28, 2011, http://archivo.elheraldo.hn/Ediciones/2011/08/29/Noticias/Honduras-sin-presencia-en-la-frontera-con-Guatemala-desde-hace-75-anos.

C. Border Security Policies and Programs at the Multilateral Level Regionally

I. SEFRO

The region's chief regional multilateral institution, the Central American Integration System (SICA),[35] manages a program called Border Security in Central America (SEFRO). SEFRO is financed almost exclusively by the European Union (EU), which aims to transfer its experience and knowledge of international integration to Central America.[36] SEFRO thus far consists mostly of a series of notional political and economic capacity-building programs, implemented by a diverse set of regional and international agencies. Central to SEFRO's regional plan is the concept of Integrated Border Management, a program framework derived from successful cases of joint-border management among EU member countries.[37]

The SEFRO program, however, faces at least three important challenges. First, the administrative structure behind it, SICA, is far weaker than the European Union, and the Central American nations lack the political stability and institutional structure needed to implement a European-style integration strategy. SICA today has no influence or voice in national policymaking and is largely irrelevant to actual regional affairs. Unless it develops legislative power and administrative capacity — that is granted by member states — such problems will continue to hinder its effectiveness and that of the SEFRO program.

Another challenge is the shortage of resources. SEFRO's budget of 6 million euros[38] is insufficient to create a working, integrated, regional border-control system, given the glaring weaknesses in the region's existing border-control efforts. Also, the program is not comprehensive; it is oriented toward improving technical capacity (e.g., the training of customs and law enforcement personnel, as well as improved communications and scanning technologies, and administrative and information-processing systems) for the monitoring and control of border transit. It does not address the complexity of social and economic life in isolated, frontier communities where markets, economies, communities, and families span unrecognized borders, and nationality is meaningless.[39]

---

35 SICA is the regional organization created by the countries of Belize, Honduras, Panama, Costa Rica, Nicaragua, El Salvador, and Guatemala in 1991 as the institutional framework for the political, social, and economic integration of Central America.
36 Efforts like this to create institutions in other regions that reflect European Union (EU) values, structures, and processes have been central to the European Union's foreign policy. See Luiña E. Fernandez, "Relaciones UE-CA: Poder Normativo en acción, Europa a través de sus espejos" (doctoral thesis, Santiago de Compostela: Inédito, 2012): 131.
37 European Union, *Programa Regional de Seguridad Fronteriza en América Central. DCI-ALA/2009/021-386* (Brussels: European Union, 2009).
38 The SEFRO budget included 5 million euros from the European Commission, and 1 million euros from SICA member governments. European Union, *Programa Regional de Seguridad Fronteriza en América Central*, 1.
39 Espach et al., *Criminal Organizations and Illicit Trafficking*, 64.

2. CARSI

The US Central American Regional Security Initiative (CARSI), initiated in 2010, is in some respects the US equivalent to SEFRO, but much larger. CARSI provides Central American nations with equipment, training, and technical assistance to support law enforcement and interdiction operations, and also supports the strengthening of the capacities of governmental institutions to address security challenges and the underlying economic and social conditions that contribute to them. CARSI spending totals approximately $100 million annually (across all of Central America, not just the three northern countries).

Thus far CARSI does not have a specific border security program, but supports a range of security policies and government programs of all types. The US government has placed, at least informally, certain conditions for CARSI funds. At a conference in Guatemala in July 2011, US Secretary of State Hillary Clinton pressed the governments of Central America to show their own commitment and seriousness by collecting more local taxes, increasing their security spending, and taking measures to strengthen the rule of law, before they could expect their full complement of US funding.

3. CFAC

Central America's Armed Forces Conference (CFAC)[40] has also made its own efforts to address border insecurity. These include bilaterally coordinated military patrols and information-sharing protocols in areas of key interest. However, due to the complicated civil-military relations in the region, these initiatives lack resources and institutional substance and are inconsistent. Governments are increasingly using their militaries to support police patrols and actions — particularly in El Salvador and Honduras — but those are national initiatives, and they complicate CFAC's goal of promoting professional militaries. The use of the military to support law enforcement efforts can cause confusion in authorities and rules of engagement, and potentially puts militaries in the position of facing criticism for human-rights abuses.[41]

4. The Trifinio Plan

The Trifinio Plan, which includes participation from El Salvador, Honduras, and Guatemala, coordinates and promotes cooperation among 45 border municipalities in the three countries for development and infrastructure projects. Though its objectives and means do not address security directly, and it does not involve any security cooperation, its efforts do support the development and institutional strength-

---

40 CFAC members are Guatemala, El Salvador, Honduras, Nicaragua, and the Dominican Republic.
41 The militaries of Guatemala and El Salvador in particular are under constant scrutiny for their human-rights-related behavior, due to the history of brutal counter-insurgency operations they carried out in the 1970s and 1980s.

ening of border cities, which can have an effect on local security. Thus far, however, the Trifinio Plan has shown few results in this area.[42]

5. Mesoamerica Project

In a similar vein, there is the broader program of the Mesoamerica Project, which includes the nations of Central America (including Belize), Colombia, and the project's lead country, Mexico. The objective of this project is to promote, politically and financially, policy coordination and joint projects for regional economic development and integration.[43] The plan's activities contribute to border security indirectly, by promoting coordination and collaboration among border communities of different countries in areas such as water treatment, resource management, and agriculture.

6. AMUPREV

The US Agency for International Development (USAID) has been supporting a similar, though not transborder, program called the Alliance of Municipalities for the Prevention of Violence in Central America (AMUPREV), one that could reasonably be extended to border communities. This program complements local security programs by supporting dialogue and the sharing of information among municipalities and the training of typically unskilled staff to run the programs. Because AMUPREV was started only recently, in 2009, its results are difficult to measure, but the initiative shows promise as an effort to strengthen citizens' security in border communities by working through local government and civil society institutions.

7. PRODESFRO

The Programa de Desarrollo Sostenible de las Poblaciones Fronterizas (PRODESFRO) is a development-oriented initiative between Mexico and Guatemala that receives little funding or attention, but which could be leveraged as a tool for tackling security problems in a broad sense in these communities. It has operated for 14 years, and is currently active in 19 Guatemalan border municipalities and 16 Mexican ones.[44] Though small and with few concrete results to point to, PRODESFRO is a good example of how governments in the region can, at times, work across borders when local communities are engaged.

---

42   Plan Trifinio (2009) includes programs of sustainable development, enviromental protection, and conflict resolution. See Plan Trifinio, *Memoria de labores 2009* (Guatemala City, Guatemala: Plan Trifinio, 2009).
43   Proyecto Mesoamérica, "Proyecto Mesoamérica," Obtenido de Vision. Accessed January 23, 2012, www.proyectomesoamerica.org/; Camila Aviña, "La frontera olvidada: seguridad y migración en México-Guatemala," *Bien común* (2010): 41, www.fundacionpreciado.org.mx/biencomun/bc173/Camila.pdf.
44   Guadalupe Vautravers Tosca, *Estudio Comparativo de la Frontera Tabasco, México-El Petén, Guatemala* (Juarez, Mexico: Universidad Juarez Autónoma de Tabasco, 2005): 142.

Two international programs at the interagency level deserve special mention for the progress they have achieved. The Central American Commission of Migration Directors succeeded at developing CA4, a system that permits citizens of any of the four northern Central American states to travel under their own national documentation. This has proven to be one of the most important advances in the region's efforts toward integration. The Central American and Caribbean Commission of Chiefs and Directors of Police (which includes participation from Haiti, the Dominican Republic, and Colombia) has managed, over its 21 years of relatively quiet existence, to implement a modest plan against organized crime that contributed directly to six important arrests in 2011.[45] Both commissions face the problem that these government positions tend to rotate quickly, limiting their consistency and continuity of effort.

VI. Recommendations for Improved Border Security Policies and Practices

Given the socioeconomic complexity of life in the border regions, and the fact that many of these communities have been without a consistent, positive state presence for generations, this chapter advocates for policies and efforts that aim to address border insecurity within the broader context of public security provision throughout these countries. Recommendations include:

A. Differentiate among the Problems of Violence, Illicit Trafficking, and Organized Crime

The current regional security strategy — supported by the United States — is unrealistic in its objective to eradicate narcotics and organized crime, and vague in its treatment of illicit trafficking, organized crime, and violence as if these were an integrated, instead of associated, set of issues. As a result, the policies and operations that derive from the strategy can be counterproductive in terms of worsening, at least in the short and medium term, the problems they are purported to resolve. The case of Mexico's war against drugs, announced in 2006, offers compelling evidence that overly militarized, aggressive efforts against organized crime in the context of weak, corrupt state institutions (particularly law enforcement and judicial systems) tend to increase violence and have uncertain effects on crime.[46]

---

45 Interview with Werner Ovalle.
46 Melissa Dell makes a well-documented and compelling case for the correlation between the new policy by the PAN government in Mexico in 2006 and an increase in violence. See Melissa Dell, *Trafficking Networks and the Mexican Drug War* (Cambridge, MA: Harvard University, 2012), http://scholar.harvard.edu/files/dell/files/121113draft.pdf.

It is important to keep in mind that illicit trafficking itself does not necessarily correlate with violence or other types of crime. The smuggling of common goods and humans, for example, flourished for decades along these borders with relatively little violence before organized-criminal groups began to fight over routes and extort money from traffickers, as well as attacking, robbing, and kidnapping migrants for ransom. Even before regional drug trafficking surged in the 2000s, homicide rates in El Salvador, Guatemala, and Honduras were several times higher than in the rest of Latin America. A geographic breakdown of recent murder rates in Guatemala shows that the most dangerous areas are in the capital and other urban areas, and that many border departments with high volumes of narco-trafficking are relatively safe. Drug-related violence tends to correlate with contention over routes and territories (both in rural and urban areas), more than with trafficking itself. Stable trafficking routes, where everyone knows who to pay, where thievery and competition are rare, and where law enforcement is effectively neutralized, tend to generate little violence.

In practice, security policies that aim to stop illicit trafficking are in some cases at odds with those that are supposed to reduce violence. The interdiction of high-value products, the breaking up of routes, and the arrests or killing of drug cartel officials, raises uncertainty among traffickers and can destabilize long-standing agreements among various organized-crime groups. In doing so, these actions only bolster opportunism and conflict among such groups. Criminal groups whose revenues from drug trafficking are suddenly reduced may turn to kidnapping, extortion, or other more violent crimes in order to make their money. To be effective in the long term, security strategies must address not only these crimes and the violence associated with them, but more importantly the underlying economic and demographic factors that reproduce more criminals, traffickers, and organized-crime groups.

Security strategies must not only aim to reduce crime and violence in the short term, but to improve public security and the rule of law over the medium and long term. Without functioning, legitimate public security institutions — from police forces to courts to prisons — backed by an accountable political system less penetrated by organized crime, any progress is likely to be only temporary.

B. Focus on Improving Security in Border Regions, instead of Border Security

Policymakers both within and from outside the region should recognize the complexity of border residents' relations with states and with borders. In many border regions, the border is immaterial as local residents thrive through buying and selling in local markets on both sides of the border. As discussed, many border communities have little or no exposure to the national government except for — in some cases — memories of military actions during the civil wars of the 1980s. The central government is distant and irrelevant to their daily concerns and affairs, and associated with corruption.[47] Residents in these communities rely a great deal on local political actors and benefactors, who in many cases may be involved with illicit trafficking, to provide public goods and help them in times of trouble.

In these cases, efforts to tighten border controls must first involve the introduction of state services into these communities and the provision of opportunities for these citizens to have livelihoods and access to what they need without crossing the border. If not, border security policies will almost certainly meet public resistance, and even if effective could cause significant economic problems in the region.

The fundamental problem in border regions is not border insecurity — it is the lack of citizen security and the rule of law. Improving state capacity for border control — through well-trained, professional agents, modern customs processes and scanning equipment, and so on — is worthwhile, but by itself will do little to stop the flood of illicit trafficking at blind crossings and elsewhere. New technologies and advanced communications and rapid response systems are expensive, difficult to maintain, and would stretch the capabilities of the region's small, under-resourced security forces.

These governments must instead improve their border security by improving security within border zones. They can do so by: (1) increasing their presence in these communities by providing services (especially effective and fair public security, criminal investigation, and judicial services) to local citizens so they come to recognize the national government as a source of protection and assistance, not just exploitation; and (2) replacing, over time, the parallel, informal systems of governance and security provision that exist alongside the formal rule-of-law institutions.

C. Create New National and Regional Security Frameworks

Border security is a task for civilian authorities and forces, which militaries can support when necessary and when sovereignty is threatened. Though militaries are becoming ever more involved in public security in these countries, governments thus far have not defined carefully, through proper legislative mechanisms, the authority and responsibilities of these forces — both police and military — and whatever measures are needed to ensure institutional accountability. Other domestic agencies must align their approaches and coordinate efforts in order to achieve efficiency and effectiveness.

---

47 Espach et al., *Criminal Organizations and Illicit Trafficking*, 80-3.

Similar alignment and coordination must take place internationally; to control a border from only one side is virtually impossible. Efforts to create national security frameworks should correspond to and support similar efforts at the regional level.

These measures will require levels of political leadership and commitment that have been lacking thus far. The United States and Mexico must be involved, but the essential leadership must come from within Central America. No government appears inclined to provide SICA with the personnel, resources, and authority it would require to succeed in leading regional reforms.

D. Improve Systems for Information Sharing and Coordination

At present, without a functioning regional security framework the countries of Central America lack information about what their neighbors are doing and what is happening in terms of crime and trafficking trends across their borders. The lack of confidence-building measures (especially outside of the military-to-military sphere, which CFAC coordinates) and the frequent cycling of security ministers and agency directors complicate the sharing of information.

A good first step would be to ensure that all border police and military posts can communicate at will with their counterparts across the border and with local municipal governments. The fact that such communication, for example, between two countries' customs agencies a few hundred meters apart, does not occur because one post does not have money in its budget for international calls, should be easily remediable.[48] At least at this level, the SEFRO program supported by EU funds could make an immediate positive impact by supplying modern, secure communications equipment to all border posts in the region.

Higher up the command chain, the lack of defined counterparts in border security efforts hinders international dialogue and coordination. The border states of Mexico, and their Guatemalan counterparts, must define a level for routine interactions on border policy and border-related information that is appropriate and effective. If it must be within the national government, it should coordinate directly with local governments as well and be accountable to them. A similar structure for cooperation must be established with the other countries of the region as well.

E. Involve Local Governments

In many of these communities the national government — including its national police — is viewed largely as a corrupt, predatory system

---

48 This anecdote was shared by Werner Ovalle.

not to be welcomed but avoided. For that reason, national governments, especially in the short and medium term, should work with and through municipal governments, which tend to have more influence locally and to better understand local needs and challenges.[49] While local governments in many cases are affected by corruption and inefficiency, at least at the local level, residents tend to understand those problems and know the actors involved. Efforts to create mechanisms for accountability and transparency can win public support at the local level because it is relatively easy to understand how they would operate. In some cases, municipal governments have been able to manage the presence of criminal organizations, including drug-trafficking cartels in their communities, and reduce their negative effects on the broader community.[50]

National governments should consider decentralizing some administrative tasks and resources related to security to those local governments, within frameworks of improved regional communication and coordination and national oversight, in order to strengthen state presence via institutions already present and active in those communities. Ultimately, a policy focus on protecting citizens instead of physical space will not eliminate smuggling and other forms of border exploitation, which are traditional elements of life in border communities, but could greatly reduce the volume and negative externalities of those illicit activities.

VII. Conclusion

The problem of border insecurity in northern Central America is not new, though recently high levels of drug trafficking and violence in the region have brought new attention to the dilemma. Rooted in long-standing regional quandaries — a paucity of resources; weak and corrupt governments; highly concentrated economies and political systems that systematically neglect rural, peripheral regions; and a lack of regional coordination — these problems will not be solved quickly. Even with the needed provision of better-trained and -equipped police, more mobile and lethally armed forces, and more modern equipment and technologies, they will not be solved overnight. Instead, the effective and universal rule of law depends on the

---

[49] At least in Guatemala, municipal governments are more representative and legitimate, in the eyes of the public, than is the national government. Electoral turnout is consistently between 9 and 13 points higher in local elections than in exclusively presidential ones. This is largely because local governments are the largest providers of social welfare in most of the country.

[50] Such is the case in Malacatán, where the community's *institutional density* reduces (though never eliminates) the social impact of organized crime (see Espach et al., *Criminal Organizations and Illicit Trafficking*, 33-63). The Guatemalan Ministry of Governance, with support from the US government, has also applied with success a model of community policing backed by improved social services aimed at youth and potential gang members in the urban communities of Mexico and Villanueva.

strengthening of state institutions and the spread of national societal demands.

Ultimately, a focus on borders *per se* is misleading. Free-market democracies do not have secure borders as much as they have a secure rule of law across their territories. Central American countries should focus their efforts on creating state presence and providing state services, especially security, within border communities, particularly those along key trafficking routes. This will require patience, political commitment, and resources across several years.

Works Cited

Anonymous. 2011. *Grupos de poder en Petén: Territorio, política y negocios.* www.libertopolis.com/wp-content/files/REPORTE_PETEN_DE_Insightcrime_Parte_I.pdf.

Arauz, Sergio. 2011. Cantidad de militares ha crecido un 57% en primer gobierno de izquierda. *El Faro*, December 7, 2011. http://elfaro.net/es/201112/noticias/6827/.

Aviña, Camila. 2010. La frontera olvidada: seguridad y migración en México-Guatemala. *Bien común*, 39-43. www.fundacionpreciado.org.mx/biencomun/bc173/Camila.pdf.

Cerna, Mario. 2011. Honduras sin presencia en la frontera con Guatemala desde hace 75 años. *El Heraldo*, August 28, 2011. http://archivo.elheraldo.hn/Ediciones/2011/08/29/Noticias/Honduras-sin-presencia-en-la-frontera-con-Guatemala-desde-hace-75-anos.

———. 2012. Falta de fondos impide terminar la demarcación. *El Heraldo*, February 13, 2012. http://archivo.elheraldo.hn/Ediciones/2011/08/24/Noticias/Falta-de-fondos-impide-terminar-la-demarcacion/.

Dell, Melissa. 2012. *Trafficking Networks and the Mexican Drug War*. Cambridge, MA: Harvard University. http://scholar.harvard.edu/files/dell/files/121113draft.pdf.

Donadio, Marcela. 2011. *Índice de Seguridad Pública y Ciudadana en América Latina. El Salvador, Guatemala y Honduras.* Argentina: Red de Seguridad y Defensa de America Latina (RESDAL). www.resdal.org/libro-seg/.

Dudley, Steven S. 2010. *Drug Trafficking Organizations in Central America: Transportistas, Mexican Cartels and Maras.* Washington, DC: Woodrow Wilson International Center for Scholars. http://stevendudley.com/pdf/Wilson%20Center%20Central%20America%20Dudley%2005%2017%2010.pdf.

EFE News Agency. 2012. Guatemala y El Salvador integrarán Policía Binacional para fronteras. *PrensaLibre*, February 13, 2012. www.prensalibre.com/noticias/politica/Guatemala-Salvador-integraran-Policia-Binacional_0_645535659.html.

Espach, Ralph, Javier Melendez, Daniel Haering, and Miguel Castillo. 2011. *Criminal Organizations and Illicit Trafficking in Guatemala's Border Communities.* Washington, DC: Center for Naval Analyses. www.cna.org/research/2011/criminal-organizations-illicit-trafficking.

European Union (EU). 2009. *Programa Regional de Seguridad Fronteriza en América Central. DCI-ALA/2009/021-386.* Brussels: European Union.

Fernandez Luiña, E. 2012. Relaciones UE-CA: Poder Normativo en acción, Europa a través de sus espejos. Doctoral thesis. Santiago de Compostela: Inédito.

Graham, Ronan. 2012. Honduras Guns Feeding Central America's Arms Trade. *Insightcrime.org*, August 12, 2012. www.insightcrime.org/news-analysis/honduras-guns-feeding-central-americas-arms-trade.

Herrera, Marizza Alejandra. 2011. *Retos y principios para el combate del crimen transnacional en regiones fronterizas: El caso de la frontera Guatemala-México.* Santiago de Chile: Centro de Estudios Estratégicos.

López, Julie. 2010. Guatemala´s Crossroads: Democratization of Violence and Second Chances. Working Paper Series on Organized Crime in Central America. Washington, DC: Woodrow Wilson International Center for Scholars. www.wilsoncenter.org/sites/default/files/Lopez.Guatemala.pdf.

Martínez, Oscar. 2011. La frontera de los Señores. *El Faro.* August 14, 2011. www.salanegra.elfaro.net/es/201108/cronicas/5018/.

Meléndez, Javier Q., Roberto B. Orozco, Sergio M. Moya, and Miguel R. López. 2010. *Una Aproximación a la Problemática de la Criminalidad Organizada en las Comunidades del Caribe y de Fronteras.* Managua, Nicaragua: Instituto de Estudios Estratégicos y Políticas Públicas.

Miroff, Nick and William Booth. 2011. Arrests of Illegal Migrants on US-Mexico Border Plummet. *The Washington Post*, December 3, 2011. www.washingtonpost.com/world/americas/arrests-of-illegal-migrants-on-us-mexico-border-plummet/2011/12/02/gIQA6Op8PO_story.html.

Ovalle, Werner. 2012. Programa de Seguridad Fronteriza para América Latina. Interviewed by Daniel Haering, January 23, 2012.

Plan Trifinio. 2009. *Memoria de labores 2009.* Guatemala City, Guatemala: Plan Trifinio.

Proyecto Mesoamérica. 2012. Proyecto Mesoamérica. Obtenido de Vision. Accessed January 23, 2012. www.proyectomesoamerica.org/.

Red de Seguridad y Defensa de America Latina (RESDAL). 2011. *Indice de Seguridad Publica y Ciudadana en America Latina.* Buenos Aires, Argentina: RESDAL.

Vautravers Tosca, Guadalupe. 2005. *Estudio Comparativo de la Frontera Tabasco, México-El Petén, Guatemala.* Juarez, Mexico: Universidad Juarez Autónoma de Tabasco.

United Nations Office on Drugs and Crime (UNODC). 2010. *World Drug Report 2010.* New York: UNODC. www.unodc.org/unodc/en/data-and-analysis/WDR-2010.html.

CHAPTER 4

HUMAN SMUGGLING AND TRAFFICKING INTO EUROPE: A COMPARATIVE PERSPECTIVE

Louise Shelley
George Mason University

I. Introduction

Human smuggling and trafficking are two of the fastest growing transnational criminal activities, and are thought to be the most lucrative forms of organized crime after the drug trade.[1] While most victims are located in Asia, Western Europe has become a major destination point. Smugglers and traffickers make substantial profits from the thousands of people who seek to enter Europe illicitly. While it is difficult to know the exact numbers — there is a lack of research and a paucity of data, particularly on trafficking — the United Nations Office on Drugs and Crime (UNODC) estimates that in 2010 there were 140,000 trafficking victims in Europe, generating $3 billion annually for their exploiters.[2] The most comprehensive study, conducted in 2005 by the International Labor Organization (ILO), estimated the global profits of commercial sex trafficking and forced labor at that time as $33.9 billion annually, based on approximately 1.4 million trafficked people engaged in commercial sexual exploitation and millions more in forced labor.[3] Almost half of these profits came from industrialized nations, a significant number of them in Europe.[4]

---

1   United Nations Office on Drugs and Crime (UNODC), *2007 UN World Drug Report* (Vienna: UNODC, 2007), www.unodc.org/pdf/research/wdr07/WDR_2007.pdf.
2   UNODC, *The Globalization of Crime: A Transnational Organized Crime Threat Assessment* (Vienna: UNODC, 2010), www.unodc.org/unodc/en/data-and-analysis/tocta-2010.html.
3   Patrick Belser, "Forced Labor and Human Trafficking, Estimating the Profits" (working paper, International Labor Organization, Geneva, March 2005): 5, 14. www.ilo.org/sapfl/Informationresources/ILOPublications/WCMS_081971/lang--en/index.htm.
4   According to UNODC there are 1.4 million trafficked migrants in Asia and the Pacific; 270,000 in industrialized countries; 250,000 in Latin America; and 230,000 in the Middle East and North Africa; UNODC, *Human Trafficking: An Overview* (Vienna: UNODC, 2008): 6, www.ungift.org/docs/ungift/pdf/knowledge/ebook.pdf.

Human trafficking and smuggling into Europe have grown since the 1980s. Emigrants are attracted by generous welfare support and perceived economic advantages, as well as the demand in Western Europe for "three-d" workers — those willing to take dirty, dangerous, and/or degrading jobs that national citizens are unwilling to do. The increase can also be attributed to a number of converging global factors in the past few decades: economic crises in Asia; the conflicts in Iraq, Afghanistan, and Pakistan; and poverty in the global south have all encouraged emigration. Finally, options for legal entry to Europe are limited. In 2011, Europe accepted approximately 1.7 million legal migrants — a small percentage of those seeking entry — from outside the European Union.[5] Meanwhile, Frontex detected 141,000 illegal border crossings during the same year.[6] In 2008 an estimated 1.9 million to 3.8 million unauthorized migrants resided in the European Union.[7] Given the numbers of people who wish to travel to the European Union, it is no surprise that the problem of human smuggling has grown relative to that of human trafficking.[8]

European policymakers have made great efforts to restrict illegal immigration. This is an enormous challenge given the nature of EU borders — the Mediterranean coast is lightly guarded, and the long border that many Eastern European countries share with the former Soviet Union is notorious for its often-corrupt border patrol personnel.[9] Given that Eastern Europe includes porous, lawless regions through which many migrants and trafficked people from other regions transit, the lack of control along this eastern border is especially significant.[10]

Combating the transnational criminal groups that facilitate trade in humans has become a high priority for the Member States of the European Union. Policymakers have allocated significant resources to Europol, the European police agency, and established Frontex, a Euro-

---

5   Eurostat, "Migration and Migrant Population Statistics," http://epp.eurostat.ec.europa.eu/statistics_explained/index.php/Migration_and_migrant_population_statistics; Kristiina Kangaspunta, "Mapping the Inhuman Trade: Preliminary Findings of the Human Trafficking Database," *Forum on Crime and Society* 3, no. 1 (2003): 81, www.unodc.org/pdf/crime/forum/forum3_note1.pdf.
6   Frontex, *Annual Risk Analysis 2012* (Warsaw: Frontex, 2012), http://frontex.europa.eu/assets/Attachment_Featured/Annual_Risk_Analysis_2012.pdf.
7   Clandestino Project, *Policy Brief: Size and Development of Irregular Migration to the EU* (Athens: Hellenic Foundation for European and Foreign Policy, 2009): 4, http://irregular-migration.net/typo3_upload/groups/31/4.Background_Information/4.2.Policy_Briefs_EN/ComparativePolicyBrief_SizeOfIrregularMigration_Clandestino_Nov09_2.pdf.
8   John Salt and Jennifer Hogarth, *Migrant Trafficking and Human Smuggling in Europe: A Review of the Evidence* (Geneva: International Organization for Migration, 2000), chapter 8.
9   Human Rights Watch, "Hopes Betrayed: Trafficking of Women and Girls to Post-Conflict Bosnia and Herzegovina for Forced Prostitution," *Human Rights Watch* 14, no. 9 (2002): 26–34, www.unhcr.org/refworld/docid/3e31416f0.html.
10 Frank Laczko, Irene Stacher, and Amanda Klekowski von Koppenfels, *New Challenges for Migration Policy in Central and Eastern Europe* (Cambridge, UK: Cambridge University Press, 2002).

pean agency devoted to border control.[11] Despite such steps, and mass media coverage of the issue, human smuggling and trafficking continue unabated. The financial crisis in 2008 only exacerbated the situation by increasing economic hardship in source countries and placing businesses in Europe under severe pressure to cut costs. According to Europol, this has increased demand for unauthorized migrants and trafficked victims in the economy as companies under financial pressure struggle to survive.[12]

This chapter reviews national reports and research conducted in diverse countries of the European Union to paint a better picture of what is taking place on the ground. It also reviews reports and analyses of cases that have been investigated by Europol, ILO, the Organization for Security and Cooperation in Europe (OSCE), and the Financial Action Task Force (FATF). Finally, it draws on the scholarly literature on smuggling and trafficking. The chapter has two goals: to outline the effects of smuggling/trafficking and to discuss policy options for limiting the phenomenon.

Definitions

Both human smuggling and trafficking involve the recruitment, movement, and delivery of migrants from a host to a destination state. What differentiates the two activities is whether the migrants are willing participants or not: traffickers enslave and exploit trafficked persons, while smuggled migrants have a consensual relationship with their smugglers and are free at the end of their journey.

The United Nations has adopted a legislative framework to define human smuggling and trafficking. Distinct protocols were adopted on the two crimes in 2000 in conjunction with the United Nations Convention against Transnational Organized Crime.[13] The adoption of these protocols in tandem with the convention reflects the international understanding that human smuggling and trafficking are part of organized crime.[14]

---

11 Letizia Paoli and Cyrille Fijnaut, "General Introduction," in *Organised Crime in Europe: Concepts, Patterns and Control Policies in the European Union and Beyond*, eds. Cyrille Fijnaut and Letizia Paoli (Dordrecht: Springer, 2004): 1. Frontex is a specialized and independent body based in Warsaw to provide operational cooperation on border issues; see Frontex, "Origin," www.frontex.europa.eu.
12 Europol, *Trafficking in Human Beings in the European Union* (The Hague: Europol, 2011), www.europol.europa.eu/sites/default/files/publications/trafficking_in_human_beings_in_the_european_union_2011.pdf.
13 Kara Abramson, "Beyond Consent, Toward Safeguarding Human Rights: Implementing the United Nations Trafficking Protocol," *Harvard International Law Journal* 44, no. 2 (2003): 473–502; Janice G. Raymond, "The New UN Trafficking Protocol," *Women's Studies International Forum* 25, no. 5 (2002): 491–502.
14 Phil Williams and Ernesto Savona, eds., *The United Nations and Transnational Organized Crime* (London and Portland, OR: Cass, 1996).

The definition of trafficking in Article 3a of the anti-trafficking protocol defines the problem in the following way:

> *The recruitment, transportation, transfer, harbouring or receipt of persons, by means of the threat or use of force or other forms of coercion, of abduction, or fraud, of deception, of the abuse of power or of a position of vulnerability or the giving or receiving of payments or benefits to achieve the consent of a person having control over another person, for the purpose of exploitation. Exploitation shall include, at a minimum, the exploitation or the prostitution of others or other forms of sexual exploitation, forced labour or services, slavery or practices similar to slavery, servitude or the removal of organs.*[15]

This broad definition of trafficking includes sex trafficking as well as trafficking into exploitative work situations such as domestic help, agricultural work, and work in dangerous industries. It also includes the trafficking of child soldiers, of children put up for adoption or forced into begging, and the less well-known and analyzed problem of organ trafficking. Most of these types of trafficking are present in Europe, though there is no evidence of child soldiers since the wars in the Balkans.

The Protocol Against the Smuggling of Migrants by Land, Sea, and Air defines the problem in the following way:

> *"Smuggling of Migrants" shall mean the procurement, in order to obtain directly or indirectly, a financial or other material benefit, of the illegal entry of a person into a State Party of which the person is not a national or a permanent resident.*[16]

Although human smuggling and trafficking have different definitions, the demarcation is not so clear in real life.[17] Because smuggling often occurs within the context of large-scale migration, there are numerous possibilities for abuse. Individuals, most often women and children, may start off as paying clients of human smugglers but end up as trafficking victims.[18]

---

15 UNODC, "United Nations Convention on Transnational Organized Crime and the 2 Protocols Thereto," www.unodc.org/unodc/en/treaties/CTOC/index.html.
16 United Nations, "Protocol Against the Smuggling of Migrants by Land, Sea, and Air, Supplementing the United Nations Convention Against Transnational Organized Crime (2000)," www.uncjin.org/Documents/Conventions/dcatoc/final_documents_2/convention_smug_eng.pdf.
17 For a discussion of this, see Bridget Anderson and Julia O'Connell Davidson, *Is Trafficking in Human Beings Demand Driven? A Multi-Country Pilot Study 9* (Geneva: International Organization for Migration, 2003), www.iom.int/jahia/webdav/site/myjahiasite/shared/shared/mainsite/published_docs/serial_publications/mrs15b.pdf.
18 Benjamin S. Buckland, "Smuggling and Trafficking: Crossover and Overlap," in *Strategies Against Human Trafficking: the Role of the Security Sector*, ed. Cornelius Friesendorf (Vienna and Geneva: National Defense Academy and Austrian Ministry of Defense and Sports, 2009): 146, 151, www.dcaf.ch/Publications/Strategies-Against-Human-Trafficking-The-Role-of-the-Security-Sector.

II. Smuggling and Trafficking: Models, Trends, and Routes

Human smuggling and trafficking are not evenly distributed across Europe. According to the United Nations, five countries of Western Europe — Belgium,[19] Germany, Greece, Italy, and the Netherlands — have recorded the highest number of trafficking victims. These same countries are also principal destinations for individuals who enlist the services of human smugglers.[20] The next-largest hubs of human trafficking are Austria, Denmark, France, Spain, and Switzerland.[21] Greece and Spain are not only recipient countries for unauthorized migrants but also have been exploited by transnational smuggling organizations because of their key geographic locations on the periphery of Europe.[22]

These destination countries are among the most affluent and populous countries in Europe. They also have large sex markets, either due to domestic demand or tourism industries (such as in the south of Spain).[23] Moreover, many have large immigrant populations, ports, and extensive coastlines that facilitate the entry of both trafficking victims and smuggled migrants.

The trafficking landscape within the European Union is diverse (as it is in other developed countries). While most of the attention has been focused on sex trafficking of women from Eastern Europe, the former Soviet Union (particularly after the fall of the Berlin Wall), and Africa, victims come from all regions of the world. UNODC reports a greater variety in the national origins of human-trafficking victims in Europe than in any other part of the world.[24]

A. Source Countries: East vs. South

Different regions of Europe receive victims from different source countries. In its 2012 assessment, Europol identified five major hubs

---

19 Stef Janssens, Patricia Le Cocq, and Koen Dewulf, *La Traite et Le Trafic des être$ humain$: Lutter avec des personnes. Et des ressources Rapport Annuel 2008* (Brussels: Centre pour l'égalité des chances et la lutte contre racisme, 2009).
20 Khalid Koser, "Why Migrant Smuggling Pays," *International Migration* 46, no. 2 (2008): 3–26; Gao Yun and Véronique Poisson, "Le trafic et l'exploitation des immigrants chinois en France" (Geneva: Organisation International du Travail, 2005): 70–2, www.ilo.org/sapfl/Informationresources/ILOPublications/WCMS_082332/lang--fr/index.htm.
21 UNODC, *Trafficking in Persons: Global Patterns* (Vienna: UNODC, 2006): 92, www.unodc.org/pdf/traffickinginpersons_report_2006-04.pdf.
22 Akis Kalaitzidis, "Human Smuggling and Trafficking in the Balkans: Is It Fortress Europe?" *Journal of the Institute of Justice and International Studies* 5 (2005): 3-4.
23 Alejandro Gómez-Céspedes and Per Stangeland, "Spain: The Flourishing Illegal Drug Haven in Europe" in *Organised Crime in Europe,* eds. Cyrille Fijnaut and Letizia Paoli (Dordrecht: Springer, 2004): 402-4.
24 UNODC, "The Globalization of Crime."

of organized crime. Each is connected to particular source countries, and specializes in certain types of labor placement. The five hubs are: in the northwest, the Netherlands and Belgium; in the northeast, the Baltic states and Kaliningrad; in the southeast, Bulgaria, Romania, and Greece; in the south, southern Italy; and in the southwest, Spain and Portugal.[25]

The southwest hub (Spain and Portugal) receives victims from the Iberian Peninsula and redistributes them throughout Europe according to market demand. Chinese victims often work in textile sweatshops, Eastern Europeans in agriculture, South Americans in the sex industry, while Roma children are forced to beg and commit thefts.[26] The southern criminal hub (southern Italy) is a transit and destination area for individuals who come from North and West Africa, Eastern Europe, the Balkans, and China.[27] They work in the textile industry, entertainment sector, elder and child care, and construction.[28]

The major source countries of smuggling and trafficking victims were identified by Europol in 2008 as Bulgaria, Moldova, Nigeria, Romania, the Russian Federation, and Ukraine. In many cases, trafficking to Europe is facilitated by members of victims' own migrant communities.[29] Identified source countries include some of the poorest nations in Europe. Meanwhile, Europol fails to mention several source countries that were once European colonies. These include Morocco and Algeria in North Africa, and Brazil, the Dominican Republic, and Colombia in Latin America. Citizens from these former colonies are increasingly identified as victims of trafficking, both for sex work and general labor, particularly in Mediterranean countries. Large numbers of women from the Dominican Republic, a Spanish colony until the early 19th century, are trafficked to Spain.[30] Women from Brazil and Colombia are increasingly identified as victims of sex trafficking in Europe.[31] Italy, home to the second-largest Nigerian dias-

---

25 Europol, *Trafficking in Human Beings in the European Union*, 12.
26 Ibid, 11-12.
27 For more on the Southern and Eastern European region see Rebecca Surtees, "Traffickers and Trafficking in Southern and Eastern Europe: Considering the Other Side of Human Trafficking," *European Journal of Criminology* 5, no. 1 (2008): 39–68.
28 Europol, *EU Organised Crime Threat Assessment (OCTA) 2011* (The Hague: Europol, 2011): 12, www.europol.europa.eu/content/press/europol-organised-crime-threat-assessment-2011-429.
29 Europol, *Annual Report 2008* (The Hague: Europol, 2008): 17–9, www.europol.europa.eu/sites/default/files/publications/annual_report_2008.pdf.
30 International Organization for Migration (IOM), Migration Information Program, *Trafficking in Women from the Dominican Republic for Sexual Exploitation* (Geneva: IOM, 1996), www.oas.org/atip/country%20specific/TIP%20DR%20IOM%20REPORT.pdf; US Department of State, "Dominican Republic," in *Trafficking in Persons Report 2009* (Washington, DC: Department of State, 2009): 123–34, www.state.gov/j/tip/rls/tiprpt/2009/123136.htm.
31 Liz Kelly, *Journeys of Jeopardy: A Review of Research on Trafficking in Women and Children in Europe* (Geneva: IOM, 2002): 26, www.iom.int/jahia/webdav/site/myjahiasite/shared/shared/mainsite/published_docs/serial_publications/mrs11b.pdf.

pora community in Europe, had 12,500 trafficked Nigerian women working as prostitutes in 2006, representing approximately half of the prostitutes in Italy.[32]

Among child victims, leading source regions are Eastern Europe, North Africa, and Asia.[33] A significant number come from the Middle East and the Indian subcontinent by way of Turkey and often the Balkans. Most of these children, defined as trafficking victims, will work in illegal labor markets, but not the sex markets that have received the most attention.[34]

The Arab Spring had a significant impact on illegal immigration into Western Europe. Many migrants from sub-Saharan Africa who were working in North Africa when the unrest started escaped to Europe. Frontex, the European border-control agency, noted that in the first nine months of 2011 there were 112,000 illegal migrants detained compared to 77,000 for the same time period in 2010, although not all from sub-Saharan Africa.[35] As routes across the Mediterranean were shut off through interdiction at sea, more individuals came through Turkey. Consequently, Greece noted an upturn in smuggled migrants.[36]

B. Routes

There are many routes into Europe from different regions of the world — North Africa, Latin America, and Eastern Europe and Asia. These routes change over time as traffickers and smugglers adapt to enforcement and effective border patrols. The accession of the Czech Republic and Poland into the European Union in 2004 reduced the use of routes across these countries, as border controls were tightened with training

---

32 John Picarelli, "Organised Crime and Human Trafficking in the United States and Western Europe," in *Strategies Against Human Trafficking: The Role of the Security Sector,* ed. Cornelius Friesendorf (Vienna: National Defense Academy and Austrian Ministry of Defense and Sport, 2009): 134; Jørgen Carling, "Trafficking in Women from Nigeria to Europe," July 2005, *Migration Information Source,* www.migrationinformation.org/Feature/display.cfm?ID=318; Jørgen Carling, *Migration, Human Smuggling and Trafficking from Nigeria to Europe* (Geneva: IOM, 2006), www.iom.int/jahia/webdav/site/myjahiasite/shared/shared/mainsite/published_docs/serial_publications/mrs23.pdf.
33 United Nations Children's Fund (UNICEF) Innocenti Research Center, *Child Trafficking in Europe: A Broad Vision to Put Children First* (Florence, Italy: UNICEF, 2008), www.unicef-irc.org/publications/pdf/ct_in_europe_full.pdf.
34 Financial Action Task Force (FATF), *Money Laundering Risks Arising from Trafficking in Human Beings and Smuggling of Migrants* (Paris: FATF and OECD, 2011): 34, www.fatf-gafi.org/dataoecd/28/34/48412278.pdf.
35 Agence France-Presse (AFP), "Arab Spring Prompts Surge of Illegal Immigrants to EU," AFP, November 16, 2011, www.timesofmalta.com/articles/view/20111116/local/arab-spring-prompts-surge-of-illegal-immigrants-to-eu.394158.
36 EurActiv, "Greece Measures Arab Spring Immigration Impact," EurActiv, November 22, 2011, www.euractiv.com/justice/greece-measures-arab-spring-immigration-impact-news-509109.

and support from the European Union. By contrast, the accession of Romania and Bulgaria to the European Union in 2007 has not been as successful in shutting off Balkan smuggling rings. These countries still suffer high levels of corruption at the borders and in law enforcement generally. Many of the routes used for humans are the same as those used for traded goods.

The primary transit routes are across the Mediterranean, the Balkans, Eastern Europe, and Turkey. The individuals trafficked into Europe usually travel by air, sea, and land (most often by cars, buses, and trucks, and not much by rail). The most recently identified route is from Macedonia, through Serbia and Hungary, and into Austria.[37] Entry from the Baltic Sea and through the northern parts of Europe is less common. Many routes — whether from Africa, China, or Afghanistan and Pakistan — are circuitous and involve long distances. The routes from Latin America are more direct; those smuggled and trafficked often fly straight to Spain or Portugal.

For migrants from Nigeria, there are many routes from the exit point of Lagos into Europe.[38] These routes change and reorganize on a constant basis to avoid intervention by the police or immigration patrol guards. During the civil conflict in Libya, new routes were used as smugglers and traffickers exploited the internal chaos in Libya to move individuals from sub-Saharan Africa to Italy's island of Lampedusa.[39] Overall, approximately 8 percent of unauthorized migrants from North Africa enter Europe by sea. And a significant number enter legally by air, then stay on beyond their visa authorization.[40]

Various types of transport are often combined. The Chinese who died in a van crossing the English Channel had been initially transported by "Snakeheads"[41] from Beijing to Belgrade. Then with the efficiency of a well-coordinated international business, they were moved by auto through Hungary, Austria, France, and the Netherlands before being

---

37 AFP, "Arab Spring Prompts Surge of Illegal Immigrants to EU."
38 The air routes include direct flights from Lagos to Italy, Lagos-France-Italy, Lagos-London-Italy, Lagos-Accra (by road)-Italy (by air), Lagos-the Netherlands-Italy, and Lagos-any Schengen country-Italy. Other land and sea routes include Lagos-Togo-Morocco-Spain-Italy, Lagos-Togo-Libya-Italy, Lagos-Togo, Morocco-Spain-France-Italy, and Lagos-Togo-Burkina Faso-Mali-Spain-France-Italy. United Nations Interregional Crime and Justice Research Institute (UNCJRI), *Trafficking of Nigerian Girls in Italy: The Data, the Stories, the Social Services* (Rome: UNCJRI, 2010), www.unicri.it/services/library_documentation/publications/unicri_series/trafficking_nigeria-italy.pdf.
39 Sabina Castelfranco, "Italian Island of Lampedusa Sees Increase of North African Refugees," Voice of America, March 7, 2011, www.voanews.com/english/news/europe/Italian-Island-of-Lampedusa-sees-Increase-of-North-African-Refugees-117510933.html.
40 UNODC, *The Role of Organized Crime in the Smuggling of Migrants from West Africa to the European Union* (Vienna: UNODC, 2011): 8, www.unodc.org/documents/human-trafficking/Migrant-Smuggling/Report_SOM_West_Africa_EU.pdf.
41 "Snakeheads" refers to smugglers who facilitate the transfer of Chinese migrants to Western countries.

loaded in a van for their last fateful leg to the United Kingdom.[42]

III. Profile of Facilitators

Traffickers are logistics specialists who can move individuals across vast distances. They often require numerous safe houses along the way where they can lodge their human cargo until it is safe to move them further. For individuals traveling the Balkan route into Western Europe, these safe houses are often in Turkey and Eastern Europe. For those traveling from sub-Saharan Africa, there are many stations along the way. Routes are often indirect, as traffickers carefully avoid policed roads, border checkpoints, and jurisdictions where there is efficient and honest law enforcement. While not quite as complex as the operations of large-scale narcotics traffickers, human traffickers and smugglers do require a military-like intelligence capacity to successfully avoid these obstacles. The end destinations for victims are often diaspora communities that can absorb the trafficked people, or urban areas where allied crime groups can receive and distribute the trafficked laborers.[43]

The barriers to entry have created an enormous variety of facilitators who assist those who seek illegal entry into the European Union.[44] They range from small groups to complex international organizations. Some of these criminals engage in only smuggling while others also traffic individuals.[45] Those who facilitate these movements are not necessarily part of criminal networks. Knowingly or unknowingly, legitimate businesses can aid in the trafficking process. Employment agencies, which may be complicit, are used to facilitate the movement of victims. Apartment owners may knowingly or unknowingly rent apartments to smuggled and trafficked individuals, thus facilitating their residence in Western Europe. Nightclub owners may employ young unauthorized female workers, and some even go to great lengths to secure such employees. Hotels seeking cheap staff may hire unauthorized workers who have been smuggled or trafficked into Europe.[46]

---

42 Joan Clements and David Sapsted, "Terror Inside the Lorry of Death, Britain' Straw Says Truck Deaths a Warning," *The Telegraph*, June 20, 2000, www.telegraph.co.uk/news/uknews/1343932/Terror-inside-the-lorry-of-death.html; Warren Hoge, "Dutch Truck Driver Sentenced in Chinese Immigrant Deaths," *New York Times*, April 6, 2001, www.nytimes.com/2001/04/06/world/dutch-truck-driver-sentenced-in-chinese-immigrant-deaths.html.
43 For example, see FATF, *Money Laundering Risks*, 35–6.
44 Shared Hope International, *DEMAND: A Comparative Examination of Sex Tourism and Trafficking in Jamaica, Japan, the Netherlands and the United States* (Vancouver, WA: Shared Hope International, 2012): 71–2, http://sharedhope.org/wp-content/uploads/2012/09/DEMAND.pdf.
45 Louise Shelley, *Human Trafficking: A Global Perspective* (Cambridge, UK: Cambridge University Press, 2010); FATF, *Money Laundering Risks*, 34.
46 Alexis Aronowitz, Gerda Theuermann, and Elena Tyurykanova, *Analysing the Business Model of Human Trafficking to Better Prevent the Crime* (Vienna: Organization for Security and Cooperation in Europe and United Nations Global Initiative to Fight Human Trafficking, 2010), http://s3.amazonaws.com/rcpp/assets/attachments/1154_osce_business_model_original.pdf.

The business of human smuggling and human trafficking is possibly more ethnically diversified in the European Union than in North America. Of various national and ethnic criminal groups, several in particular are associated with the trafficking of human beings. Nigerian and Chinese groups are probably the most threatening to society, according to a 2011 Europol assessment.[47] Bulgarian, Romanian, and Roma criminal groups are also particularly active, as are Albanian, Russian, Turkish, and Hungarian groups. Such criminal groups — especially the Chinese, Nigerian, and Romanian ones — work with diaspora communities overseas to limit detection. Bulgarian, Hungarian, and Turkish groups are often facilitators, moving individuals from the east through the Balkans to Western Europe. Balkan traffickers operate within family groups, often functioning within diaspora communities. For example, French police discovered through wiretaps that a sister of a French-based Balkan trafficker was operating a cell in Belgium.[48] But such groups also hire individuals outside their communities to reduce suspicions. Belgian and Dutch women have been hired by Balkan clans to help run day-to-day operations and minimize risks.[49]

Women are more active in human trafficking than other areas of transnational crime.[50] That said, they still number less than half of traffickers. According to a UN analysis of identified offenders in Europe, women rarely compose more than one-third of identified suspects in human-trafficking cases. Minors have been suspected as traffickers in some Western European countries. The majority of identified traffickers work within their own countries, but in some countries the presence of foreign traffickers is much higher.[51]

A. Criminal Groups from Turkey and the Balkans

Turkish criminal groups have become specialists in the logistics needed to move drugs and people. Groups in the eastern parts of Turkey, especially on the borders with Iraq and Syria, have helped facilitate this illicit trade.[52] In some cases, the crime groups are linked with the terrorist organization the Kurdish Workers' Party (PKK).[53] Data from the

---

47 Europol, *Trafficking in Human Beings in the European Union*, 20.
48 Jana Arsovska and Stef Janssens, "Human Trafficking and Policing: Good and Bad Practices," in *Strategies against Human Trafficking: The Role of the Security Sector*, ed. Cornelius Friesendorf (Vienna: National Defense Academy and Austrian Ministry of Defense and Sport, 2009), 213.
49 Ibid, 184.
50 Dina Siegel and Sylvia de Blank, "Women Who Traffic Women: The Role of Women in Human Trafficking Networks — Dutch Cases," *Global Crime* 11, no. 4 (2010): 436–47; Alexis Aronowitz, *Human Trafficking, Human Misery: The Global Trade in Human Beings* (Westport, CT: Praeger, 2009): 52–5.
51 UNODC, *Global Report on Trafficking in Persons* (Vienna: UNODC, 2009): 56, www.unodc.org/unodc/en/human-trafficking/global-report-on-trafficking-in-persons.html.
52 Mark Galeotti, "Turkish Organized Crime: Where State, Crime, and Rebellion Conspire," *Transnational Organized Crime* 4, no.1 (1998): 25–42.
53 Janssens, Le Cocq, and Dewulf, *La Traite et Le Trafic des être$ humain$*.

Organized Crime and Smuggling section of the Turkish National Police reveal that many transnational criminals from different countries are now operating in Turkey, facilitating this trade. In 2008 criminals from 64 different countries operating in conjunction with different Turkish crime groups were arrested in Turkey.[54] Many of these were functioning in the drug arena, but their networks were also utilized for trade in human beings.

Turkish human smuggling follows the trade routes of the Ottoman Empire. Instead of bringing spices and silks from the Orient to Western Europe, these routes bring political refugees from conflicts in Afghanistan, Iraq, Pakistan, and Somalia and labor migrants who seek to the earn more in the economies of Europe. Turkish organized crime has globalized in recent decades, facilitating this trade from East to West.[55] The geographic location of Turkey on the Black Sea and its borders with Soviet successor states Iraq, Syria, and Iran all facilitate this trade. Moreover, its long Mediterranean border — too long to be fully policed — provides excellent points of covert entry and exit from the country.

Turkish diaspora communities play a central role in human trafficking for labor exploitation, with some members collaborating with Turkish crime groups — either voluntarily or as a result of coercion. Because these networks are strong in the United Kingdom, Belgium, the Netherlands, Germany, and elsewhere in Western Europe, Turkish groups can effectively smuggle individuals into Western Europe, where their labor can be exploited.[56]

The now dismantled Balkan human trafficking ring Tara, which had 52 participants identified through regional coordination, reveals the complexities of illegally transporting large numbers of people across different borders. Four criminal groups, each in a different country, cooperated to move at least 192 people from the Near and Far East, charging those seeking to enter the European Union 1,000 to 1,500 euros each. The Croatian newspaper *Dalje* reports:

> *The smugglers were very careful about their business, trying to cover up their tracks by all means, i.e., to stay below the radar. The groups from Croatia were connected with smugglers from other countries. The persons transported across the border with regular transport lines, in personal vehicles, taxis or vans. The persons were accommodated at secret locations before the transport and payments were conducted via*

---

54 Turkish National Police, *Turkish Organized Crime Report* (Ankara: Department of Anti-Smuggling and Organized Crime, 2008).
55 Stef Janssens and Jana Arsovska, "People Carriers: Human Trafficking Networks Thrive in Turkey," *Jane's Intelligence Review* (December 2008): 44–7; Xavier Raufer, "Une maffya symbiotique: traditions et évolutions du crime organisé en Turquie," *Sécurité Global*, 10 (2009-10): 91–119.
56 Frank Bovenkerk and Y. Yucel Yesilgoz, "The Turkish Mafia and the State," in *Organized Crime in Europe*, eds. Cyrille Fijnaut and Letizia Paoli (Dordecht, The Netherlands: Springer, 2004): 585–603; Janssens, Le Cocq, and Dewulf, *La Traite et Le Trafic des être$ humain$*.

messengers — drivers of regular bus routes or Western Union... The arrested criminals often used illegal border crossings and a guide.[57]

B. The Role of Corruption

Corruption is deeply connected to the problem of human trafficking in Europe: travel agencies, border guards, customs officials, consular officers, and other diplomatic personnel must be bribed or extorted for trafficking to be successful.[58] This problem is not confined to Eastern Europe and other transit countries where corruption levels are known to be high. As illustrated below, corruption in Western European embassies overseas has also facilitated human trafficking.

The high levels of corruption in transit countries aid greatly in facilitating the movement of people. Turkish law enforcement investigations of human smuggling have disclosed that corruption facilitates this trade not only in sending countries, but also among law enforcement officials in the Balkans.[59] For example, in the mid-1990s a former senior Bulgarian intelligence official opened a travel agency in Bulgaria. By establishing close relations with the embassy of a Western European state in Sofia, official tourist visas were delivered en masse to the travel agency for travel to Western Europe. This allowed the agency to facilitate human smuggling and trafficking, activities it combined with money laundering.[60]

Similar problems have been documented for the Swiss embassy in Pakistan. In 2006 Swiss officials in the Department of Foreign Affairs reported that criminal gangs "involved in human trafficking had almost certainly infiltrated the visa section of the Islamabad embassy and corrupted officials." As in the Bulgarian case, Pakistani travel agencies were complicit in the visa fraud.[61] In the same time period, a Belgian employed in the protocol service of the Belgian Ministry of Foreign Affairs arranged the distribution of diplomatic passports and "sold

---

57 For a discussion of the case, see Southeast European Law Enforcement Center (SELEC), "52 Persons Detained in 4 Countries during Operation 'TARA' Joint Investigation Supported by the SECI Center," (press release, SELEC, April 3, 2009), www.secicenter.org/p450/02+April+2009. For the specific quote, see *Dalje*, "Smuggled 200 people to EU via Croatia," *Dalje*, April 2, 2009, www.javno.com/en-croatia/smuggled-200-people-to-eu-via-croatia_248077.
58 John Pomfret, "Bribery At Border Worries Officials" *Washington Post*, July 15, 2006, www.washingtonpost.com/wp-dyn/content/article/2006/07/14/AR2006071401525.html; Transparency International, "Corruption and Human Trafficking" (working paper #3/2011, Transparency International, Berlin, 2011), www.transparency.org/whatwedo/pub/working_paper_corruption_and_human_trafficking.
59 Interview by the author with a police official assigned to the organized-crime branch in Konya, Turkey, in March 2008.
60 Arsovska and Janssens, "Human Trafficking and Policing," 190.
61 Leslie Holmes, "Corruption and Trafficking: Triple Victimisation?" in *Strategies Against Human Trafficking: The Role of the Security Sector*, ed. Cornelius Friesendorf (Vienna: National Defense Academy and Austrian Ministry of Defense and Sport, 2009): 103.

at least 300 residence permits to people associated with the Russian mafia. One of the accomplices in this case was an important figure in a large Russian company engaged in money laundering."[62]

In Senegal press reports reveal that in at least two different cases, officials in embassies of Western European countries were engaged in the selling of visas. This corrupt activity has possibly allowed the admission of thousands of people to EU Member States over the years.[63] Corruption does not only occur at the borders or the consulates and embassies of European countries overseas. It also takes place on the street, as police are paid to look the other way and not probe brothels or target labor or sex traffickers.[64]

IV. Profile of Trafficked and Smuggled Persons

Smuggled and trafficked individuals work in many different sectors of the economy. According to a 2012 UN study, 62 percent of victims in Europe and Central Asia are trafficked for sexual exploitation. Of those individuals who are trafficked for other types of work, most perform menial jobs that do not require specialized training. As many as 29 percent of trafficked victims in some Western and Central European countries are working in forced labor.[65] Most are men, but some are women and children. Exploitation in the construction sector and in restaurants, bars, and small-scale production is particularly common.[66] Trafficked and smuggled individuals also commonly work in agriculture and fisheries. Domestic servitude, a highly concealed phenomenon, often occurs within ethnic diaspora communities: young girls and women are forced to work long hours and sometimes confined to the homes where they work.[67] Overall, trends on the national level vary. The 2012 UN study highlighted a particularly high percentage of trafficked domestic servitude victims in Austria, where a nongovernmental organization (NGO) reported that 15 percent of its trafficked victims fell in this category. In the Netherlands, these victims accounted for 2 percent of those helped by a local NGO.[68]

---

62 Arsovska and Janssens, "Human Trafficking and Policing," 190.
63 UNODC, *The Role of Organized Crime in the Smuggling of Migrants from West Africa to the European Union*, 11.
64 Holmes, "Corruption and Trafficking."
65 UNODC, *Global Report on Trafficking in Persons* (Vienna: UNODC, 2012), www.unodc.org/documents/data-and-analysis/glotip/Trafficking_in_Persons_2012_web.pdf.
66 FATF, *Money Laundering Risks*, 14, 32–56.
67 Europol, *Trafficking in Human Beings in the European Union*; Organization for Security and Cooperation in Europe (OSCE), *Unprotected Work, Invisible Exploitation: Trafficking for the Purpose of Domestic Servitude* (Vienna: OSCE, 2010): 13–9, www.childtrafficking.com/Docs/osce_10_unprotected_work_0411.pdf.
68 UNODC, *Global Report on Trafficking in Persons*, 2012, 56.

Authoritative sources on trafficking in European countries reveal an enormous range of victims: young children who are forced to sell flowers in the street, beg, or commit petty crime for their traffickers; mature women who are exploited as care providers for children and the elderly; and men forced to undertake manual labor.[69]

There are many types of individuals who can be classified as trafficking victims under European law and who work in countries throughout Europe. A detailed ILO study of the approximately 50,000 Chinese individuals illegally in France reveals that many working in restaurants and small factories could be trafficking victims.[70] Smuggled Chinese are also exploited in Italian sweatshops to keep the Italian textile industry competitive. Trafficked workers in southern Italy harvest agricultural products at prices that keep these products competitive.[71] In 2004 Operation Marco Polo led to the arrest of 91 traffickers and 571 accomplices who supplied more than 600 businesses with more than 3,200 Chinese laborers in Italy.[72]

Khalid Koser's research on Pakistanis smuggled into the United Kingdom reveals that these individuals are primarily working in restaurants and other service industries.[73] In 2004 at least 21 Chinese cockle pickers died in the United Kingdom after being trapped in rising tides — evidence of the exploitation of smuggled workers.[74] French parliamentary hearings almost a decade ago focused on the problem of children, primarily from Africa, trafficked into domestic servitude.[75] The same problem is now reported in Spain, involving Angolan children.[76] Well-developed Brazilian networks bring irregular workers to Portugal, where they are distributed for labor exploitation to construction sites throughout Western Europe.[77]

---

69 Kristiina Kangaspunta, "Trafficking in Persons Global Patterns," (presentation at International Symposium on International Migration and Development, UNODC, Turin, June 28-30, 2006): 20, www.un.org/esa/population/migration/turin/Turin_Statements/KANGASPUNTA.pdf; Europol, *Trafficking in Human Beings in the European Union*.
70 Yun and Poisson, "Le trafic et l'exploitation des immigrants chinois en France," 70–2.
71 See a video documenting the experiences of migrants from Africa and Eastern Europe harvesting oranges in southern Italy: Link TV, "Orange Harvest: The Human Cost," www.linktv.org/video/7381/orange-harvest-the-human-cost.
72 John T. Picarelli, "Enabling Norms and Human Trafficking," in *Crime and the Global Political Economy, International Political Economy Yearbook 16*, ed. H. Richard Friman (Boulder and London: Lynne Rienner, 2009): 97; Government of Italy, "Operation Marco Polo: An Investigation of the Illegal Trade in Asian Traditional Medicine," www.cites.org/common/cop/13/inf/E13i-45.pdf.
73 Koser, "Why Migrant Smuggling Pays."
74 British Broadcasting Corporation (BBC), "Cockle Pickers Died from Drowning," June 22, 2004, http://news.bbc.co.uk/2/hi/uk_news/england/lancashire/3827623.stm.
75 Assemblée Nationale, *L'esclavage, en France, aujourd'hui, Report No. 3459, Tome II, Auditions, Vol.1*, Paris, 2001, Les Documents d'information de l'assemblée nationale (Documents of the National Assembly).
76 Europol, *Trafficking in Human Beings in the European Union*.
77 FATF, "Money Laundering Risks," 34.

A UN study that focuses on sex trafficking suggests that most victims are adult females.[78] But there are male victims, too. Research conducted on the trafficking of Ukrainian and Belarusian men reveals that they are trafficked both for labor and sexual exploitation.[79] And research in Germany shows that some men from Bulgaria and Romania, often of Roma origin, are forced by traffickers to sell themselves on the streets of German cities.[80]

Significant differences are found between smuggled and trafficked people. Those who are smuggled must pay for their transport, and so often derive from the more economically privileged sets of society.[81] Of Pakistanis smuggled to the United Kingdom, for example, many have some amount of higher education but cannot find jobs commensurate with their skills at home. (Most will encounter the same fate in the United Kingdom, though for relatively higher wages.) Yet this generalization does not apply to all cases. In 2006 and 2007 many who crossed to the Canary Islands from Africa were fishermen or from fishing communities. According to one study, 58 percent had never gone to school and only half were literate.[82]

In contrast, trafficking victims are often from the "weakest social and economic groups in their countries of origin."[83] Yet there are differences among the trafficked populations. Women who come from the former Soviet Union and Eastern Europe have higher levels of education than women who are trafficked from Africa and Latin America, where there is much less access to education.[84]

The number of exploited children is not large but still numbers in the thousands. Many minors travel unaccompanied to Western Europe, most often from Eastern Europe, North Africa, and Asia.[85] In the early 2000s in Belgium alone, more than 1,000 cases were recorded of minors, primarily from Asia and Eastern Europe, transiting through Belgium to the United Kingdom to find work, unite with family, or escape a difficult situation.[86] Children trafficked into Europe may suffer

---

78   Kangaspunta, "Trafficking in Persons."
79   IOM, "Trafficking of Men — A Trend Less Considered — The Case of Belarus and Ukraine" (IOM Migration Series No. 36, IOM, Geneva, 2008), www.iom.int/jahia/webdav/site/myjahiasite/shared/shared/mainsite/published_docs/serial_publications/MRS-36.pdf.
80   Christophe Gille, "Romanians and Bulgarians in Male Street Sex Work in German Cities" (working paper, Comparative European Social Studies, Metropolitan University London), 37–59, www.aksd.eu/download/Rom__Bulg_in_German_Male_Sex_Work_Gille_2007.pdf.
81   Julie Kaizen and Walter Nonneman, "Irregular Migration in Belgium," *International Migration* 45, no. 2 (2007): 121–46; Koser, "Why Migrant Smuggling Pays."
82   UNODC, *The Role of Organized Crime*, 16.
83   Kaizen and Nonneman, "Irregular Migration in Belgium," 138.
84   Shelley, *Human Trafficking*.
85   UNICEF, "Child Trafficking in Europe."
86   Ilse Derluyn and Eric Broekaert, "On the Way to A Better Future: Belgium as Transit Country for Trafficking and Smuggling of Unaccompanied Minors," *International Migration* 43, no. 4 (2005): 31.

severe abuse. They do not enjoy the protections that are available to native-born Western European children, who generally have access to the extensive social welfare systems of the region. Children trafficked into Europe have been exploited by pedophiles; forced to become prostitutes, domestic servants, sweatshop workers, or beggars; and made to engage in petty or violent crime.[87]

With demand exceeding supply, the preponderance of European prostitutes are migrants, many of them trafficked. About 70 percent of all sex workers across Western, Southern, and Northern Europe are migrants, with significant national-level variations. In Italy, Spain, Austria, and Luxembourg, migrants comprise 80 to 90 percent of the sex-worker population; in Finland, the Netherlands, Belgium, Germany, France, Greece, Denmark, and Norway, they comprise 60 to 70 percent. In the new EU countries of Central Europe, by contrast, only 16 to 18 percent of sex workers are migrants.[88] Among trafficking victims in West and Central Europe between 2005 and 2006, 32 percent were from the Balkans, 19 percent from the former Soviet Union, 13 percent from South America, and 5 percent from Africa.[89]

Giving some sense of the scale of the problem is the fact that in Italy alone, 11,500 foreign trafficking victims working in prostitution entered a state-supported assistance program between 2000 and 2006.[90] The identified victims are only a fraction of the women trafficked into Italy. An Italian trafficking specialist suggested that at least 100 different ethnic groups were engaged in prostitution in that country with many diverse transnational crime groups involved.[91] Other European countries, lacking extensive assistance programs, are unable to identify their trafficked women. The percentage of prostitutes who are foreign born varies between 50 and 90 percent in countries for which data are available. The highest percentage of foreign-born sex workers was found in Ireland, where it reached as high as 90 percent in 2008, before the economic collapse.[92] In Norway

---

87 UNICEF, "Child Trafficking in Europe." There is much concern about the disproportionate trafficking of Roma children. See Europol, *Trafficking in Human Beings in the European Union*.
88 European Network for HIV/STI Prevention and Health Promotion among Migrant Sex Workers (TAMPEP), *Sex Work in Europe: A mapping of the prostitution scene in 25 European countries* (Amsterdam: TAMPEP International Foundation, 2009): 16, http://tampep.eu/documents/TAMPEP%202009%20European%20Mapping%20Report.pdf.
89 UNODC, *Trafficking in Persons to Europe for Sexual Exploitation*, 3.
90 Niki Kitsantonis, "In Greece, Female Sex Victims Become Recruiters," *New York Times*, January 29, 2008, www.iht.com/articles/2008/01/29/europe/traffic.php.
91 Picarelli, "Enabling Norms and Human Trafficking," 97.
92 The Ireland data come from a private communication from Nusha Yunkova, anti-trafficking coordinator, Immigrant Council of Ireland, September 12, 2008, discussing a report that her organization was preparing on human trafficking. The calculation of 40 percent for Greece was made in the late 1990s; see Gabriella Lazardis, "Trafficking and Prostitution: The Growing Exploitation of Migrant Women in Greece," *European Journal of Women's Studies* 8, no. 1 (2001): 80–1; Netherlands data come from Shared Hope International, *DEMAND*.

foreign women constitute 70 percent of the prostitution market. Native-born Norwegian prostitutes are generally older, as they are able to work under better conditions than those who have been forced into prostitution.[93] Those forced into prostitution do not have access to medical care and are forced to work outside in the extreme cold.

Some children — most often from Latin America, the former Soviet Union, and Asia — are trafficked for adoption by parents in Western Europe, who pay high fees to secure desired babies.[94] In Southeast Asia and within the Roma communities in France, Greece, and Bulgaria, pregnant women have been trafficked to secure their babies after birth.[95]

V. Impacts of Smuggling and Trafficking

The consequences of human smuggling and trafficking include reduced quality of governance as a result of corruption, violence against individual victims, and increased anti-immigrant sentiment. The last, in turn, has had a significant impact on domestic politics in Europe and has limited the possibility of integrating victims of trafficking after their identification. The diversification of organized crime into the business of human smuggling and trafficking has garnered significant profits, further embedding crime into the economic life of European countries.

Not only do the practices of smugglers and traffickers violate basic human rights, but, once arrived, the unauthorized status of the immigrants so transported challenges democratic processes. The significant numbers of unauthorized immigrants, including trafficked people, now living and working in Europe do not enjoy the rights of citizenship or legal residency. Few countries in Europe are willing to regularize their status or provide residence permits, since this could be seen as rewarding illegal behavior.[96] The result is structural inequality

---

93 Anette Brunovskis and Guri Tyldum, *Crossing Borders: An Empirical Study of Trans-National Prostitution and Trafficking in Human Beings* (Oslo, Norway: FAFO, 2004): 115, www.fafo.no/pub/rapp/426/index.htm.
94 Ethan B. Kapstein, "The Baby Trade," *Foreign Affairs* 82 (2003): 115–25; David M. Smolin, "Child Laundering: How the Intercountry Adoption System Legitimizes and Incentivizes the Practices of Buying, Trafficking, Kidnapping, and Stealing Children," *Wayne Law Review* 52 (2006): 113–200.
95 Assemblée Nationale, *L'esclavage, en France, aujourd'hui*, Report No. 3459; Niki Kitsantonis and Matthew Brunwasser, "Baby Trafficking is Thriving in Greece, *International Herald Tribune,* December 19, 2006, www.nytimes.com/2006/12/19/world/europe/19iht-babies.3951066.html; Focus News Agency, "Bulgaria and Greece Smash Baby Trafficking Network," Focus News Agency, January 25, 2011, www.flarenetwork.org/learn/project_echo/italy/article/bulgaria_and_greece_smash_baby_trafficking_network.htm.
96 Cornelius Friesendorf, ed., *Strategies against Human Trafficking: The Role of the Security Sector* (Vienna and Geneva; National Defense Academy and Austrian Ministry of Defense and Sport, 2009): 444–510.

between citizens and legal residents on the one hand, and unauthorized migrants on the other.

The illegal status of trafficking victims also has concrete consequences for the victims. In the legalized sex markets of Europe, legal residents and native-born prostitutes have health benefits, the protections of labor laws, and pension benefits. Trafficked women, meanwhile, go unprotected. The same can be said of smuggled workers, who enjoy none of the benefits of European labor laws. They may work double the hours of authorized European workers and in unsafe and unregulated work conditions, with no health protections and for often inadequate wages.

The problem of human smuggling and trafficking in Europe is further impacted by the ambivalent relationship between states and victims. European countries, for example, have fewer protections for victims of trafficking than does the United States. In many European countries, women are given temporary visas to help in the prosecution of their cases but are provided no long-term assurance of staying in Europe, as the T (for trafficking) visa provides in the United States. In other words, the victims are helped only as long as they are useful to the state in its prosecution of the perpetrators. Most states only provide financial and support services to victims who aid criminal investigators but there are not provisions for those who have been victimized and manage to escape their traffickers. Those who are returned home often face renewed victimization either by their families, their communities, and/or their traffickers.[97]

Although Europe has lower levels of violence than many regions in the world, the presence of human traffickers and smugglers increases the level of intrapersonal violence. Because much of this violence occurs within closed communities where individuals are exploited in industries under the radar, it remains unreported to law enforcement and often stays off official registries. Although the violence among organized-crime groups has diminished in recent years,[98] this decline refers to intragroup conflicts. Meanwhile, female and child trafficking victims silently suffer high levels of abuse. *Stolen Smiles*, a study conducted in Great Britain, found that trafficked women suffered extreme physical abuse.[99] In Belgium today, according to the research of Jana Arsovska, pimps have been known to brand trafficked women's vaginas to ensure that ownership is known and the women cannot escape their control.[100]

---

97 Ibid.
98 Pino Arlacchi, *L'inganno e la paura. Il mito del caos globale* (Milan : Il Saggiatore, 2009).
99 Cathy Zimmerman, Mazeda Hossain, Kate Yun, Brenda Roche, Linda Morison, and Charlotte Watts, *Stolen Smiles: A Summary Report on the Physical and Psychological Health Consequences of Women and Adolescents Trafficked in Europe* (London: London School of Hygiene and Tropical Medicine, 2006): 10–22, www.lshtm.ac.uk/php/ghd/docs/stolensmiles.pdf.
100 Jana Arsovska, "Albanian Organized Crime, Past and Present: Changing Operational Methods and Organizational Structures," (presentation at annual meeting of the American Society of Criminology, Washington, DC, November 16, 2012).

The violence and human-rights abuses are transnational, as criminal investigations reveal. The Sneep Case, an investigation of a large trafficking organization in the Netherlands, showed that perpetrators committed violence across borders to intimidate any victims willing to cooperate with Dutch investigators. In that case the home of a victim from the Czech Republic was burned to ensure she would not testify against her traffickers. Human smuggling and trafficking, meanwhile, have resulted in multiple deaths in Europe. The previously cited case of the Chinese immigrants killed while crossing the English Channel is but one example. The transnational and covert nature of human-trafficking networks has made it difficult for European authorities to dismantle them. There have been very few arrests or prosecutions of those engaged in the smuggling and trafficking of other humans.[101]

VI. Policy Response: Looking Forward

There is no single strategy that will stem the growth of human trafficking, but there are several ways to discourage it:

Address demand. Demand for both trafficked women and forced labor must be reduced. This comes through education and prevention, prosecution, and a political will to terminate labor and sexual exploitation. It requires the participation of not only governments but also the private sector and civil society.

Target consumers and businesses. A successful anti-trafficking strategy must involve consumers, business people, and vulnerable communities. Those who avail themselves of the services of trafficked people, and the businesses that facilitate this trade, must become more central to countertrafficking policies. This involves raising awareness. The International Organization for Migration (IOM) launched a media campaign in late 2009 urging consumers to buy responsibly. This campaign goes beyond fair trade; it seeks to bring those working in the informal sector in developing countries under the protection of labor laws, and to ensure greater control of product supply chains.[102]

Yet, more is needed than words. A stick is required to impose financial, reputational, and legal penalties on those who exploit others. At the same time there must also be a carrot that incentivizes corporations

---

101 Shelley, *Human Trafficking*, Conclusion; Rudolf E. H. Hilgers, "The Programmatic Approach of Trafficking in Human Beings in the Netherlands," (presentation at The Commodification of Illicit Flows: Labour Migration, Trafficking and Business, Centre for Diaspora and Transnational Studies, University of Toronto, October 9-10, 2009).
102 *Global Eye on Human Trafficking*, "What's Behind the Things We Buy?" *Global Eye on Human Trafficking*, Issue 7, October 2009, 1–2, www.iom.int/jahia/webdav/site/myjahiasite/shared/shared/mainsite/projects/showcase_pdf/global_eye_seventh_issue.pdf; Interview by the author with Richard Danziger, head of countertrafficking at IOM, who is behind this campaign, November 20, 2009, Dubai.

and others to counter trafficking by providing above-board employment, jobs, and proper due diligence. Citizens must recognize the human consequences of purchasing goods or services that depend on trafficking for their provision.

Address policy discrepancies. Many policymakers suggest that tackling the problem of human trafficking requires harmonization of laws, from specific prostitution laws to trafficking and immigration policy more generally. Harmonization, however, must occur *between* as well as *within* countries. As it is, national approaches vary greatly. In the Netherlands, legalizing prostitution and ensuring that brothels have legal workers will, it is hoped, control trafficking. Sweden, on the other hand, has outlawed the purchase of sex in efforts to control both domestic prostitution and trafficking. The danger is that trafficked migrants will simply be displaced from Sweden to the Netherlands.

Decrease profits. More attention needs to be paid to the financial aspects of human smuggling and trafficking. At the present time, too few steps are being taken to either follow the profits of exploitation or deprive smugglers and traffickers of those profits. With high demand and promising profits, there is little disincentive.

Improve labor laws. Last but not least, migration policies need to be revised to allow for the legal movement of workers to supply sectors of the European economy for which workers are needed. Labor demand will be an acute problem in Europe as long as birth rates remain low. Without policies that can provide for more legal migration, the problems of human smuggling and trafficking will continue despite efforts to secure borders.

Works Cited

Abramson, Kara. 2003. Beyond Consent, Toward Safeguarding Human Rights: Implementing the United Nations Trafficking Protocol. *Harvard International Law Journal* 44 (2): 473–502.

Agence France-Presse (AFP). 2011. Arab Spring Prompts Surge of Illegal Immigrants to EU. November 16, 2011. www.timesofmalta.com/articles/view/20111116/local/arab-spring-prompts-surge-of-illegal-immigrants-to-eu.394158.

Anderson, Bridget and Julia O'Connell Davidson. 2003. *Is Trafficking in Human Beings Demand Driven? A Multi-Country Pilot Study 9*. Geneva: International Organization for Migration. www.iom.int/jahia/webdav/site/myjahiasite/shared/shared/mainsite/published_docs/serial_publications/mrs15b.pdf.

Arlacchi, Pino. 2009. *L'inganno e la paura: Il mito del caos globale*. Milan: Il Saggiatore.

Aronowitz, Alexis. 2009. *Human Trafficking, Human Misery: The Global Trade in Human Beings*. Westport, CT: Praeger.

Aronowitz, Alexis, Gerda Theuermann, and Elena Tyurykanova. 2010. *Analysing the Business Model of Human Trafficking to Better Prevent the Crime*. Vienna: Organization for Security and Cooperation in Europe (OSCE) and United Nations Global Initiative to Fight Human Trafficking (UN GIFT). http://s3.amazonaws.com/rcpp/assets/attachments/1154_osce_business_model_original.pdf.

Arsovska, Jana. 2012. Albanian Organized Crime, Past and Present: Changing Operational Methods and Organizational Structures. Presentation at annual meeting, American Society of Criminology, Washington, DC, November 16, 2012.

Arsovska, Jana and Stef Janssens. 2009. Human Trafficking and Policing: Good and Bad Practices. In *Strategies Against Human Trafficking: The Role of the Security Sector*, ed. Cornelius Friesendorf. Vienna: National Defense Academy and Austrian Ministry of Defense and Sport.

Assemblée Nationale. 2001. *L'esclavage, en France, aujourd'hui*. Report No. 3459, Tome II, Auditions, Vol. 1. Paris: Assemblée Nationale.

Belser, Patrick 2005. Forced Labor and Human Trafficking, Estimating the Profits. Working paper, International Labor Organization, Geneva, March 2005. www.ilo.org/sapfl/Informationresources/ILOPublications/WCMS_081971/lang--en/index.htm.

Bovenkerk, Frank and Yucel Yesilgoz. 2004. The Turkish Mafia and the State. In *Organized Crime in Europe*, eds. Cyrille Fijnaut and Letizia Paoli. Dordrecht: Springer.

British Broadcasting Corporation (BBC). 2004. Cockle Pickers Died from Drowning. http://news.bbc.co.uk/2/hi/uk_news/england/lancashire/3827623.stm.

Brunovskis, Anette and Guri Tyldum. 2004. *Crossing Borders: An Empirical Study of Trans-National Prostitution and Trafficking in Human Beings*. Oslo, Norway: Fafo. www.fafo.no/pub/rapp/426/index.htm.

Buckland, Benjamin S. 2009. Smuggling and Trafficking: Crossover and Overlap. In *Strategies Against Human Trafficking: The Role of the Security Sector*, ed. Cornelius Friesendorf. Vienna and Geneva: National Defense Academy and Austrian Ministry of Defense and Sports. www.dcaf.ch/Publications/Strategies-Against-Human-Trafficking-The-Role-of-the-Security-Sector.

Carling, Jørgen. 2005. Trafficking in Women from Nigeria to Europe. *Migration Information Source*, July 2005. www.migrationinformation.org/Feature/display.cfm?ID=318.

———. 2006. *Migration, Human Smuggling and Trafficking from Nigeria to Europe*. Geneva: IOM. www.iom.int/jahia/webdav/site/myjahiasite/shared/shared/mainsite/published_docs/serial_publications/mrs23.pdf.

Castelfranco, Sabina. 2001. Italian Island of Lampedusa Sees Increase of North African Refugees. Voice of America, March 7, 2011. www.voanews.com/english/news/europe/Italian-Island-of-Lampedusa-sees-Increase-of-North-African-Refugees-117510933.html.

Clandestino Project. 2009. *Policy Brief: Size and Development of Irregular Migration to the EU*. Athens: Hellenic Foundation for European and Foreign Policy. http://irregular-migration.net/typo3_upload/groups/31/4.Background_Information/4.2.Policy_Briefs_EN/ComparativePolicyBrief_SizeOfIrregular-Migration_Clandestino_Nov09_2.pdf.

Clements, Joan and David Sapsted. 2000. Terror Inside the Lorry of Death, Britain's Straw Says Truck Deaths a Warning. *The Telegraph*, June 20, 2000. www.telegraph.co.uk/news/uknews/1343932/Terror-inside-the-lorry-of-death.html.

Dalje. 2009. Smuggled 200 People to EU via Croatia. *Dalje*, April 2, 2009. www.javno.com/en-croatia/smuggled-200-people-to-eu-via-croatia_248077.

Derluyn, Ilse and Eric Broekaert. 2005. On the Way to A Better Future: Belgium as Transit Country for Trafficking and Smuggling of Unaccompanied Minors. *International Migration* 43 (4): 31.

EurActiv. 2011. Greece Measures Arab Spring Immigration Impact. EurActiv, November 22, 2011. www.euractiv.com/justice/greece-measures-arab-spring-immigration-impact-news-509109.

Europol. 2008. *Annual Report 2008*. The Hague: Europol. www.europol.europa.eu/sites/default/files/publications/annual_report_2008.pdf.

———. 2011. *EU Organised Crime Threat Assessment (OCTA) 2011*. The Hague: Europol. http://migrantsatsea.files.wordpress.com/2011/05/octa_2011-11.pdf.

———. 2011. *Trafficking in Human Beings in the European Union*. The Hague: Europol. www.europol.europa.eu/sites/default/files/publications/trafficking_in_human_beings_in_the_european_union_2011.pdf.

Financial Action Task Force (FATF). 2011. Money Laundering Risks Arising from Trafficking in Human Beings and Smuggling of Migrants. Paris: FATF and Organization for Economic Cooperation and Development. www.fatf-gafi.org/dataoecd/28/34/48412278.pdf.

Friesendorf, Cornelius, ed. 2009. *Strategies against Human Trafficking: The Role of the Security Sector*. Vienna: National Defense Academy and Austrian Ministry of Defense and Sport.

Focus News Agency. 2011. Bulgaria and Greece Smash Baby Trafficking Network. Focus News Agency, January 25, 2011. www.flarenetwork.org/learn/project_echo/italy/article/bulgaria_and_greece_smash_baby_trafficking_network.htm.

Galeotti, Mark. 1998. Turkish Organized Crime: Where State, Crime, and Rebellion Conspire. *Transnational Organized Crime* 4 (1): 25–42.

Gille, Christophe. 2007. Romanians and Bulgarians in Male Street Sex Work in German Cities. Working paper, Comparative European Social Studies, Metropolitan University London, September 2007. www.aksd.eu/download/Rom_Bulg_in_German_Male_Sex_Work_Gille_2007.pdf.

Gómez-Céspedes, Alejandra and Per Stangeland. 2004. Spain: The Flourishing Illegal Drug Haven in Europe. In *Organised Crime in Europe,* eds. Cyrille Fijnaut and Letizia Paoli. Dordrecht: Springer.

Government of Italy. Undated. Operation Marco Polo: An Investigation of the Illegal Trade in Asian Traditional Medicine. www.cites.org/common/cop/13/inf/E13i-45.pdf.

Hilgers, Rudolf. 2009. The Programmatic Approach of Trafficking in Human Beings in the Netherlands. Presentation at The Commodification of Illicit Flows: Labour Migration, Trafficking and Business, Centre for Diaspora and Transnational Studies, University of Toronto, Canada, October 9-10, 2009.

Hoge, Warren. 2001. Dutch Truck Driver Sentenced in Chinese Immigrant Deaths. *New York Times*, April 5, 2001. www.nytimes.com/2001/04/06/world/dutch-truck-driver-sentenced-in-chinese-immigrant-deaths.html.

Holmes, Leslie. 2009. Corruption and Trafficking: Triple Victimisation? In *Strategies Against Human Trafficking: The Role of the Security Sector,* ed. Cornelius Friesendorf. Vienna: National Defense Academy and Austrian Ministry of Defense and Sport.

Human Rights Watch. 2002. Hopes Betrayed: Trafficking of Women and Girls to Post-Conflict Bosnia and Herzegovina for Forced Prostitution. Human Rights Watch 14, no. 9 (D): 26–34. www.unhcr.org/refworld/docid/3e31416f0.html.

International Organization for Migration (IOM). 2008. Trafficking of Men — A Trend Less Considered: The Case of Belarus and Ukraine. IOM Migration Series No. 36. www.iom.int/jahia/webdav/site/myjahiasite/shared/shared/mainsite/published_docs/serial_publications/MRS-36.pdf.

_____. 2009. Unaccompanied Minors within the European Union. Global Eye on Human Trafficking, Issue 7, October 2009. www.iom.int/jahia/webdav/site/myjahiasite/shared/shared/mainsite/projects/showcase_pdf/global_eye_seventh_issue.pdf.

_____. 2009. What's Behind the Things We Buy? Global Eye on Human Trafficking, Issue 7, October 2009. www.iom.int/jahia/webdav/site/myjahiasite/shared/shared/mainsite/projects/showcase_pdf/global_eye_seventh_issue.pdf.

IOM, Migration Information Program. 1996. *Trafficking in Women from the Dominican Republic for Sexual Exploitation.* Geneva: IOM. www.oas.org/atip/country%20specific/TIP%20DR%20IOM%20REPORT.pdf.

Janssens, Stef and Jana Arsovska. 2008. People Carriers: Human Trafficking Networks Thrive in Turkey. *Jane's Intelligence Review* (December 2008): 44–47.

Janssens, Stef, Patricia Le Cocq, and Koen Dewulf. 2009. *La Traite et Le Trafic des être$ humain$: Lutter avec des personnes. Et des ressources Rapport Annuel 2008*. Brussels: Centre pour l'égalité des chances et la lutte contre racisme.

Kaizen, Julie and Walter Nonneman. 2007. Irregular Migration in Belgium. *International Migration* 45 (2): 121–46.

Kalaitzidis, Akis. 2005. Human Smuggling and Trafficking in the Balkans: Is It Fortress Europe? *Journal of the Institute of Justice and International Studies* 5 (2005): 1-10.

Kangaspunta, Kristiina. 2003. Mapping the Inhuman Trade: Preliminary Findings of the Human Trafficking Database. *Forum on Crime and Society* 3 (1 and 2): 81. www.unodc.org/pdf/crime/forum/forum3_note1.pdf.

_____. 2006. Trafficking in Persons: Global Patterns. Presentation at International Symposium on International Migration and Development, UNODC, Turin, Italy. www.un.org/esa/population/migration/turin/Turin_Statements/KANGASPUNTA.pdf.

Kaplan, Robert D. 2005. *Balkan Ghosts: A Journey through History*. New York: Picador.

Kapstein, Ethan B. 2003. The Baby Trade. *Foreign Affairs* 82: 115–25.

Kitsantonis, Niki. 2008. In Greece, Female Sex Victims Become Recruiters. *New York Times*, January 29, 2008. www.iht.com/articles/2008/01/29/europe/traffic.php.

Kitsantonis, Niki and Matthew Brunwasser. 2006. Baby Trafficking is Thriving in Greece. *International Herald Tribune*, December 19, 2006. www.nytimes.com/2006/12/19/world/europe/19iht-babies.3951066.html.

Kelly, Liz. 2002. *Journeys of Jeopardy: A Review of Research on Trafficking in Women and Children in Europe*. Geneva: IOM. www.iom.int/jahia/webdav/site/myjahiasite/shared/shared/mainsite/published_docs/serial_publications/mrs11b.pdf.

Koser, Khalid. 2008. Why Migrant Smuggling Pays. *International Migration* 46 (2): 3–26.

Laczko, Frank, Irene Stacher, and Amanda Klekowski von Koppenfels. 2002. *New Challenges for Migration Policy in Central and Eastern Europe*. Cambridge, UK: Cambridge University Press.

Lazardis, Gabriella. 2001. Trafficking and Prostitution: The Growing Exploitation of Migrant Women in Greece. *European Journal of Women's Studies* 8 (1): 80–81.

Link TV. Undated. Orange Harvest: The Human Cost. www.linktv.org/video/7381/orange-harvest-the-human-cost.

Organization for Security and Cooperation in Europe (OSCE). 2010. *Unprotected Work, Invisible Exploitation: Trafficking for the Purpose of Domestic Servitude*. Vienna: OSCE. www.childtrafficking.com/Docs/osce_10_unprotected_work_0411.pdf.

Paoli, Letizia and Cyrille Fijnaut. 2006. General Introduction. In *Organised Crime in Europe: Concepts, Patterns and Control Policies in the European Union and Beyond*, eds. Cyrille Fijnaut and Letizia Paoli. Dordrecht: Springer.

Picarelli, John T. 2009. Enabling Norms and Human Trafficking. In *Crime and the Global Political Economy, International Political Economy Yearbook* 16, ed. H. Richard Friman. Boulder, CO: Lynne Rienner.

_____. 2009. Organised Crime and Human Trafficking in the United States and Western Europe. In *Strategies Against Human Trafficking: The Role of the Security Sector,* ed. Cornelius Friesendorf. Vienna: National Defense Academy and Austrian Ministry of Defense and Sport.

Pomfret, John. 2006. Bribery At Border Worries Officials. *Washington Post*, July 15, 2006. www.washingtonpost.com/wp-dyn/content/article/2006/07/14/AR2006071401525.html.

Raufer, Xavier. 2010. Une maffya symbiotique: traditions et évolutions du crime organisé en Turquie. *Sécurité Global,* 10 (2009-2010): 91–119.

Raymond, Janice G. The New UN Trafficking Protocol. *Women's Studies International Forum* 25 (5): 491–502.

Salt, John and Jennifer Hogarth. 2000. *Migrant Trafficking and Human Smuggling in Europe: A Review of the Evidence*. Geneva: IOM.

Salt, John and Jeremy Stein. 1997. Migration as a Business: The Case of Trafficking. *International Migration* 35 (4): 467-94.

Southeast European Law Enforcement Center (SELEC). 2012. 52 Persons Detained in 4 Countries during Operation "TARA" Joint Investigation Supported by the SECI Center. Press release, SELEC, April 3, 2009. www.secicenter.org/p450/02+April+2009.

Shared Hope International. 2007. 'Facilitators' Netherlands and Japan. In *DEMAND: A Comparative Examination of Sex Tourism and Trafficking in Jamaica, Japan, the Netherlands and the United States*, 71–72. http://sharedhope.org/wp-content/uploads/2012/09/DEMAND.pdf.

Shelley, Louise. 2010. *Human Trafficking: A Global Perspective.* New York and Cambridge, UK: Cambridge University Press.

Siegel, Dina and Sylvia de Blank. 2010. Women Who Traffic Women: The Role of Women in Human Trafficking Networks — Dutch Cases. *Global Crime* 11 (4): 436–47.

Smolin, David M. 2006. Child Laundering: How the Intercountry Adoption System Legitimizes and Incentivizes the Practices of Buying, Trafficking, Kidnapping, and Stealing Children. *Wayne Law Review* 52: 113–200.

Surtees, Rebecca. 2008. Traffickers and Trafficking in Southern and Eastern Europe: Considering the Other Side of Human Trafficking. *European Journal of Criminology* 5 (1): 39–68.

Transparency International. 2011. Corruption and Human Trafficking. Working Paper #3/2011, Transparency International, Berlin. www.transparency.org/whatwedo/pub/working_paper_corruption_and_human_trafficking.

Turkish National Police. 2008. *Turkish Organized Crime Report*. Ankara: Department of Anti-Smuggling and Organized Crime.

US Department of State. 2009. Dominican Republic. In *Trafficking in Persons Report 2009*. Washington, DC: Department of State. www.state.gov/j/tip/rls/tiprpt/2009/123136.htm.

United Nations (UN). 2000. Protocol against the Smuggling of Migrants by Land, Sea, and Air, Supplementing the United Nations Convention Against Transnational Organized Crime. www.uncjin.org/Documents/Conventions/dcatoc/final_documents_2/convention_smug_eng.pdf.

United Nations, Interregional Crime and Justice Research Institute (UNCJRI). 2010. *Trafficking of Nigerian Girls in Italy: The Data, the Stories, the Social Services.* Rome: UNCJRI. www.unicri.it/services/library_documentation/publications/unicri_series/trafficking_nigeria-italy.pdf.

United Nations Children's Fund (UNICEF) Innocenti Research Center. 2008. Child Trafficking in Europe: A Broad Vision to Put Children First. Florence, Italy: UNICEF. www.unicef-irc.org/publications/pdf/ct_in_europe_full.pdf.

United Nations, Office on Drugs and Crime (UNODC). 2006. *Trafficking in Persons: Global Patterns.* Vienna: UNODC. www.unodc.org/pdf/traffickinginpersons_report_2006-04.pdf.

_____. 2007. *UN World Drug Report 2007.* Vienna: UNODC. www.unodc.org/pdf/research/wdr07/WDR_2007.pdf.

_____. 2008. Human Trafficking: An Overview. Vienna: UNODC. www.ungift.org/docs/ungift/pdf/knowledge/ebook.pdf.

_____. 2009. *Global Report on Trafficking in Persons.* Vienna: UNODC. www.unodc.org/unodc/en/human-trafficking/global-report-on-trafficking-in-persons.html.

_____. 2010. *The Globalization of Crime: A Transnational Organized Crime Threat Assessment.* Vienna: UNODC. www.unodc.org/unodc/en/data-and-analysis/tocta-2010.html.

_____. 2011. *The Role of Organized Crime in the Smuggling of Migrants from West Africa to the European Union.* Vienna: UNODC. www.unodc.org/documents/human-trafficking/Migrant-Smuggling/Report_SOM_West_Africa_EU.pdf.

_____. 2012. *Global Report on Trafficking in Persons.* Vienna: UNODC. www.unodc.org/documents/data-and-analysis/glotip/Trafficking_in_Persons_2012_web.pdf.

_____. 2012 United Nations Convention on Transnational Organized Crime and the 2 Protocols Thereto. www.unodc.org/unodc/en/treaties/CTOC/index.html.

Väryrynen, Raimo. 2003. Illegal Immigration, Human Trafficking, and Organized Crime. Conference on Poverty, International Migration and Asylum, World Institute for Development Economics Research, United Nations University, Helsinki, Finland. www.wider.unu.edu/publications/working-papers/discussion-papers/2003/en_GB/dp2003-072/_files/78091733799863273/default/dp2003-072.pdf.

Williams, Phil and Ernesto Savona, eds. 1996. *The United Nations and Transnational Organized Crime.* London: Frank Cass.

Yun, Gao and Véronique Poisson. 2005. *Le trafic et l'exploitation des immigrants chinois en France.* Geneva: Organisation International du Travail. www.ilo.org/sapfl/Informationresources/ILOPublications/WCMS_082332/lang--fr/index.htm.

Zimmerman, Cathy, Mazeda Hossain, Kate Yun, Brenda Roche, Linda Morison, and Charlotte Watts. 2006. *Stolen Smiles: A Summary Report on the Physical and Psychological Health Consequences of Women and Adolescents Trafficked in Europe.* London: London School of Hygiene and Tropical Medicine. www.lshtm.ac.uk/php/ghd/docs/stolensmiles.pdf.

CHAPTER 5

NORTH AMERICA'S BORDERS: FINDING THE FUTURE

Brian Grant
Migration Policy Institute

Christopher Sands
Hudson Institute

I. Introduction

In the space of little more than a decade, the North American borders have been transformed out of all recognition. Before 9/11, trucks loaded with goods flowed relatively unencumbered across these borders: auto parts moved daily from one part of the production chain in Canada to another in the United States, and manufactured goods moved from factories in Mexico to US markets. Most travelers driving between Canada and the United States needed to produce no documentation or even to give their names at the border.

September 11, 2001 changed all that. The relaxed cross-border flow of people living along the border was suddenly interrupted. People living in border towns, some of them split across two countries, found their daily practice of moving from one side of the border to the other much more complicated. Business and industry, particularly in Canada, complained about a "thickening" of borders as procedural delays slowed shipments, increased costs, and, ultimately, made businesses less competitive. In fact, the US-Canada border — once almost invisible as a result of the free trade agreements of 1989 and 1994 — had become a significant obstacle to trade.

The US-Mexico border, long viewed as a threat mainly because of the illegal migration of Mexicans and Central Americans, also fell under the long shadow of suspicion that stretched out from the terrible incidents of 9/11. The walls, either physical or procedural, were being fortified.

In the second decade after 9/11, there is a growing recognition among policymakers that the recent approach to border management needs to be reframed. Public safety remains a primary concern, but not to the exclusion of economic vitality. Responding to this tough and complex challenge will require a fundamental and mainstream reconceptualization of the border — something that should have been prompted by 9/11. It will also need perspectives from beyond government and from the experts who have historically defined how borders work. But first, a look at where we have been.

II. Smart Border Accord Action Plan

In Ottawa in October 2001, President George W. Bush's administration proposed a "perimeter approach" to securing the region against future attacks: harmonizing screening procedures and seamlessly sharing intelligence between US and Canadian officials. Bush suggested this for both strategic and practical reasons: namely, that it would be faster to set up and cheaper than expanding border facilities and personnel. Prime Minister Jean Chrétien rejected this idea as likely to alarm Canadians and therefore politically difficult. The US fallback position, as expressed by the Bush administration's actions through 2005, was to cooperate with Canada where possible in its efforts to "push the border out."

In December 2001 the Canadian and US governments released the Smart Border Declaration and Action Plan. This 30-point plan was divided into four pillars: (1) securing the flow of people; (2) securing the flow of goods; (3) investing in secure infrastructure; and (4) coordination and information sharing in the enforcement of these objectives.[1]

Not surprisingly perhaps, coming as it did so quickly after the terrorist attacks, the plan offered little new thinking but was a generally ameliorative effort to mitigate (and in some cases obviate, through cooperation) the impact of US border reinforcements on trade and travel. Many of the items in the border plan were already underway and some had even been publicly announced; other initiatives, which had been pushed forward for inclusion in the plan, in the end resulted in little real progress. With a few exceptions, the plan displayed a strategy of incremental improvements, with the dominant themes of sharing more information and improving cooperation.

Complaints about a "thickening" of the border initially came from Canadian businesses, and later from Canadian policymakers. The action

---

1   Government of Canada and the United States Government, "Specifics of Secure and Smart Border Action Plan," December 2001, http://georgewbush-whitehouse.archives.gov/news/releases/2002/01/20020107.html.

plan's goal of "a border that securely facilitates the free flow of people and commerce; a border that reflects the largest trading relationship in the world,"[2] seemed to Canadians to have been lost somewhere in implementation. Support for a new approach, a Plan B, grew on the Canadian side of the border.

III. The US-Mexico Border Partnership Agreement and Action Plan

The impact of 9/11 on US-Mexico border relations was dramatic. Just days before the terrorist attacks, on September 5, 2001, the full Cabinets of the two countries met in Washington. President Bush and Mexican President Vicente Fox announced a framework for Cabinet-level negotiations that would to lead to a major bilateral deal on immigration. The agreement, which Mexican Foreign Minister Jorge Castañeda called "the whole enchilada," was to address four aspects: (1) legalization for most unauthorized Mexicans in the United States; (2) improved border enforcement; (3) a Mexico-specific temporary worker program; and (4) a public-private partnership to invest in the development of communities of origin in Mexico.[3] Six days later the deal was dead.

In March 2002 the two countries signed a much-reduced agreement to secure the border. Modeled on the earlier US-Canada "smart border" plan, the action plan laid out 22 initiatives to support three goals: (1) strengthen infrastructure; (2) facilitate the secure flow of people; and (3) ease the safe flow of goods.[4] And like the agreement with Canada, the details of the southern action plan amounted to incremental improvements to the established approach of investment in infrastructure (including technology), better cooperation, and more information sharing. This was augmented in 2004 by the signing of two more agreements: the US-Mexico Action Plan for Cooperation and Border Safety; and a Memorandum of Understanding on the Safe, Orderly, Dignified

---

2   Quoted in Testimony of Stephen E. Flynn, Commander, US Coast Guard (ret.), and Jeane J. Kirkpatrick, Senior Fellow in National Security Studies at the Council on Foreign Relations, before the Senate Committee on Foreign Relations, *U.S.-Mexico: Immigration Policy & The Bilateral Relationship*, 108th Cong., 2d sess., March 23, 2004, www.aila.org/content/default.aspx?docid=10427.
3   Marc R. Rosenblum, *Obstacles and Opportunities for Regional Cooperation: The US-Mexico Case* (Washington, DC: Migration Policy Institute, 2011), www.migrationpolicy.org/pubs/usmexico-cooperation.pdf.
4   Government of Mexico and the US Government, "Specific Measures that Comprise Joint Action Plan with Mexico," March 2002, http://georgewbush-whitehouse.archives.gov/infocus/usmxborder/01.html.

and Humane Repatriation of Mexican Nationals.[5]

IV. The Security and Prosperity Partnership

Bush and Fox, along with Canadian Prime Minister Paul Martin, announced the Security and Prosperity Partnership (SPP) at the North American Leaders Summit in Waco, Texas in March 2005. A trilateral agreement was a significant development, as was the recognition that borders are part of a complex system that permeates many aspects of North American life, not least its prosperity. The three leaders stated that the new partnership would

> implement common border security and bioprotection, [enhance surveillance] strategies, enhance critical infrastructure protection, implement a common approach to emergency response, implement improvements in aviation and maritime security, combat transnational threats, enhance intelligence partnerships, promote sectoral collaboration in energy, transportation, financial services, technology, and other areas to facilitate business, [and] reduce the costs of trade.[6]

One of the more interesting features of the SPP was the inclusion of the private sector in the discussion, following the creation of the North American Competitiveness Council (NACC) in March 2006.[7] The council brought together 30 corporate representatives from North America's largest companies. Putting business on the table was important because it created the potential to broaden the discussion beyond a narrow focus on additional procedures and investment in security hardware. While it would be nice to think that this opening of the discussion to other perspectives was the work of the three governments, the creation of the council was in fact the result of a strong push by the US Chamber of Commerce that led the Bush administration to agree that if business was able to organize itself, then a government-

---

5   *Inter alia*, these two agreements were commitments by the two governments to work more collaboratively on border security issues by establishing a US-Mexico Coordinating Commission to implement the action plan and a US-Mexico Repatriation Technical Working Group. See US Department of Homeland Security (DHS), "Fact Sheet: U.S.-Mexico Bilateral Meeting" (news release, February 20, 2004), www.hsdl.org/?view&did=478530; and Government of Mexico and US Government, "Memorandum of Understanding on the Safe, Orderly, Dignified and Humane Repatriation of Mexican Nationals," February 27, 2004, www.ice.gov/doclib/foia/repatriation-agreements/memo-of-understanding-safe-orderly-dignified-humane-repatriation-of-mexican-nationals.pdf.
6   Government of Canada, "Leaders' Statement: Security and Prosperity Partnership of North America Established" (statement delivered in Waco, Texas, March 23, 2005), www.spp-psp.gc.ca/eic/site/spp-psp.nsf/eng/00057.html.
7   Council of the Americas, "North American Competitive Council," Undated. www.as-coa.org/north-american-competitiveness-council.

private-sector dialogue could begin. With the support of its Canadian and Mexican counterparts, the US Chamber of Commerce put together a council. The council held several meetings, including a private meeting with the three leaders, and made a number of recommendations regarding greater economic integration within North America. Members of the nongovernmental organization (NGO) community, which had not pushed as strongly for inclusion as the private sector, were upset at what they saw as their exclusion from the discussions.[8]

One important development associated with the SPP was the establishment of the North American Leaders Summit (NALS). The three countries hosted NALS in rotation: Waco, 2005; Cancun, 2006; Montebello, 2007; New Orleans, 2008; and Guadalajara, 2009. Leaders changed throughout the cycle, and their successors continued to participate. Fox hosted the Cancun summit, and his successor, Felipe Calderón, began attending in Montebello. Martin attended the Waco meeting, and Prime Minister Stephen Harper hosted the Montebello summit. Bush attended his final summit in New Orleans, and President Barack Obama attended his first in Guadalajara.

At Guadalajara, Obama agreed with his counterparts that the SPP, like many initiatives associated with the Bush administration, had become a target of sharp public criticism. The leaders agreed to formally end the partnership.[9] The SPP left behind few traces. Government websites have been taken down, for example, making research on the initiative — beyond the conspiracy theories of those who felt they had been deliberately excluded from the process — extremely difficult.[10]

One legacy of the SPP, however — the NALS meetings — continues in one form or other. It was to be Canada's turn to host the follow-up to the Guadalajara summit, but the Harper government gave priority

---

[8] These disaffected civil-society groups came from all three countries and included, *inter alia*: the Council of Canadians, Fathers for Justice Canada, Stop the North American Union, the Minutemen Project, and the Mexican Action Network on Free Trade. As noted, the Security and Prosperity Partnership (SPP) was an innovative deviation from traditional trade negotiation models as it deliberately favored the involvement of private organizations and civil society in negotiations. Nonconsultation and exclusion of NGOs from the North American Competitiveness Council (NACC) was seen as a breach of this model. For further information, see Greg Anderson and Christopher Sands, *Negotiating North America: The Security and Prosperity Partnership* (Washington, DC: Hudson Institute, 2007), www.hudson.org/files/pdf_upload/HudsonNegotiatingNorthAmericaadvanceproof2.pdf.

[9] The SPP was replaced by a more limited regional agenda and a leader-driven, top-down approach. For further analysis of this see Christopher Sands, *The Canada Gambit: Will it Revive North America* (Washington, DC: Hudson Institute, 2011), www.hudson.org/files/publications/Canada%20Gambit%20Web.pdf.

[10] For example, the Council of Canadians saw SPP as a genuine threat to the principle of open government; the Minutemen Project saw SPP as a worrying step towards open immigration from Mexico to the United States; and the Mexican Action Network on Free Trade felt generally excluded from the process. For more information, see Stephen Clarkson, *Does North America Exist? Governing the Continent after NAFTA and 9/11* (Toronto: University of Toronto Press, 2008), 42-3.

to plans for hosting the G8 and G20 summits in Ontario in July 2010, and offered a North American meeting as a sidebar (since Obama was attending both, and since Mexico participates in G8+5 as well as the G20). The White House objected that this would keep Obama out of Washington for too long and requested an alternate date, but the calendar was already too full by then. The United States was open to Canada hosting in 2011, but Canada did not take up the offer, and instead Obama organized a North American leaders meeting during the Asia-Pacific Economic Cooperation (APEC) summit in Honolulu. (This meeting occurred late in the year, in a year that the United States would ordinarily have hosted). When Calderón could not attend due to the sudden death (in a helicopter crash) of his minister of public safety, Obama organized a White House meeting instead on April 2, 2012, where the three leaders renewed their trilateral dialogue.

Yet the leaders could not agree on whether further talks should be conducted on a bilateral or trilateral basis. The United States, under both the Bush and Obama administrations, favored a trilateral approach. Canada sought to re-bilateralize border discussions believing that it would be possible to advance more quickly without chaining the discussions to issues unique to the Mexican border that were politically sensitive in the United States. Thus the issue of borders was included in the final declaration of the North American Leaders' Summit 2012,[11] but only to reference previously announced, bilateral agreements, to which the chapter turns next. The language of the declaration emphasized the leaders' mutual commitment to pursuing a dual-track approach to North America's borders, referring to the "mutually-reinforcing goals of these important initiatives."

---

11   The declaration stated: "Continued North American competitiveness requires secure supply chains and efficient borders. We remain committed to achieving this through cooperative approaches. To this end, the United States and Mexico released the Declaration Concerning Twenty-first Century Border Management in May 2010 and the United States and Canada released the Beyond the Border Action Plan: A Shared Vision for Perimeter Security and Economic Competitiveness in December 2011. We are committed to the mutually-reinforcing goals of these important initiatives and to their full implementation. By also supporting the work of multilateral organizations to foster improved collaboration, integration, and standards, we better identify and interdict threats before they reach our borders, as well as expedite the legitimate movement of goods and people throughout North America in a more efficient, secure, and resilient manner. We also have instructed our trade and commerce ministers to identify sectors where we can deepen our regional cooperation through increased trade and investment." For the full statement, see The White House, "Joint Statement by North American Leaders," (press release, April 2, 2012), www.whitehouse.gov/the-press-office/2012/04/02/joint-statement-north-american-leaders.

V. The 21ˢᵗ Century Border

The seeming loss of enthusiasm for a North American vision of security and prosperity marked by the demise of the SPP did not deter Mexico's pursuit of an immigration deal with the United States. On May 19, 2010, Presidents Obama and Calderón announced a "Declaration Concerning Twenty-First Century Border Management," commonly referred to as "The 21ˢᵗ Century Border."

This new strategy was built on five key areas or themes: (1) security (which dealt with drugs and thugs, but also included responses to pandemics); (2) border infrastructure and trade facilitation (which encompassed the Global Entry program, preclearance, and transborder trucking — a longstanding irritant for Mexico); (3) energy efficiency and security; (4) economic growth and well-being (including issues related to the labor market and the problem of unauthorized migrants); and finally, (5) a more general agreement to improve cooperation on regional and global issues.

The process of articulating a bilateral way forward for the United States and Canada took longer; finally, in February 2011, President Obama and Prime Minister Harper announced a new strategy for approaching the now-linked interests of security and the economy. The full title of the new initiative was Beyond the Border: a Shared Vision for Perimeter Security and Economic Competitiveness. The declaration spoke about the need to contribute to the "economic security and well-being of both Canada and the United States," a recognition that the solution had to go beyond just fortifying the border against terrorist threats.[12]

In December 2011, the two leaders announced two action plans: the Action Plan on Perimeter Security and Economic Competitiveness and the Action Plan on Regulatory Cooperation. The first, referred to as the Border Action Plan, focused on five areas of cooperation: "addressing threats early; trade facilitation, economic growth and jobs; cross-border law enforcement; critical infrastructure and cyber-security; and managing our new long-term partnership."[13]

Under these five headings the two countries identified a list of 33 initiatives to be undertaken, along with dates for reporting back to leaders during 2012.[14] While some of these initiatives have an element

---

12 The White House, "Declaration by President Obama and Prime Minister Harper of Canada - Beyond the Border," (press release, February 4, 2011), www.whitehouse.gov/the-press-office/2011/02/04/declaration-president-obama-and-prime-minister-harper-canada-beyond-bord.
13 Government of Canada and US Government, "Beyond the Border: A Shared Vision for Perimeter Security and Economic Competitiveness" (December 7, 2011), www.dhs.gov/xlibrary/assets/wh/us-canada-btb-action-plan.pdf.
14 Ibid.

of precision in terms of deliverables and timelines — a sign, perhaps, that they are already well-advanced — many of them remain vague and speculative at this point.[15]

VI. Report Card: A Dozen Years Later

So where does North America stand a dozen years after al-Qaeda redefined the US approach to border security? It is probably fair to say that the outcome has been mixed. There are clearly more resources now engaged in enforcement activities at borders and, as a result, an increased vigilance among those seeking entry. The direct cost of this enhancement has been significant: in the many billions of dollars. But a full assessment of the first decade must also include indirect costs: the burden to people and companies using the border, the overwhelming majority of whom are legitimate, many of them conducting important cross-border trade. In a recent study, researchers John Mueller and Mark G. Stewart put the total cost for the decade — which includes "enhanced direct expenditures" and "opportunity costs" — at over $1 trillion for the United States alone.[16] A more conservative estimate of costs, by Steven Globerman and Paul Storer, found significant decreases in the value of bilateral US-Canadian trade, particularly Canadian exports to the United States.[17] Whether such costs were prudent remains an open question. What seems more evident is that even as governments continue to invoke facilitation of movement as a priority, there has been little improvement.[18]

It is surprising to note the lack of coherence among the three North American countries either at the strategic or at the operational level: there is no continental vision for the border, no trilateral declaration of intent, and no guiding narrative. The one brief flirtation with a trilateral vision — the Security and Prosperity Partnership — has ended, and the three countries are now back to conducting parallel discussions, the details of which are basically identical. It is hard to put one's finger on why a bilateral approach is preferred. For Canada and Mexico, a good bilateral deal is probably sufficient to meet their needs, although Mexican President Enrique Peña Nieto has made public overtures to both Canada and the United States to work more closely with Mexico. For the United States, a trilateral agreement would seem to make more sense, if only for the fact that it would eliminate the duplica-

---

15 Ibid.
16 John Mueller and Mark G. Stewart, *Terror, Security and Money: Balancing the Risks, Benefits, and Costs of Homeland Security* (Oxford: Oxford University Press, 2011).
17 Steven Globerman and Paul Storer, *The Impacts of 9/11 on Canada-U.S. Trade* (Toronto: University of Toronto Press, 2008).
18 For a review of post-9/11, border security initiatives on the US-Canadian border, see Christopher Sands, *Toward a New Frontier: Improving the U.S.-Canadian Border* (Washington, DC: Brookings Institution, 2009), www.brookings.edu/~/media/research/files/reports/2009/7/13%20canada%20sands/0713_canada_report.pdf.

tion of effort. For this to happen, however, Mexico probably needs to demonstrate significant improvement in the capacity and reliability of its intelligence and enforcement community, which for the moment is stretched in trying to deal with narco-traffickers.

The language used in the various declarations certainly reveals a desire to find a common guiding narrative, but so far the implementation details fall short of the aspirational tone suggested by "The 21st Century Border" and "Beyond the Border." This is not to belittle the importance of the individual improvements being proposed; for the most part, they are sound and necessary steps. But even solid, visible improvements to the two borders do not reflect the fundamental shift that 9/11 introduced. The real success of the terrorists was their ability to bypass borders (both immigration and civil aviation security), and to shake confidence and disrupt seats of power — the same goal that underlies the current threat of cyber-attacks. Fortifying old ramparts (i.e. physical borders) will not, in effect, protect the United States from its modern enemies.

VII. Moving Forward: The Power of Identity

Most of the activity since 9/11 has involved incremental changes to initiatives already in place: sharing information, introducing new procedures and new requirements, and assigning more resources to the border. Meanwhile, slowly and more or less out of sight of the public, a new direction is being mapped out. There are three key elements of this mapping.

First, there is a lot more going on in terms of screening flights than the public sees. The United States is undoubtedly the leader in air-travel screening. Analysts gather and analyze information from several sources, using increasingly sophisticated software, to provide intelligence to support officers working the lines. This intelligence has improved border screening — i.e. the determination of who is admissible to the country and who represents a threat — but it has not done much to ease the flow of legitimate traffic.

The second element is provided by frequent-traveler enrollment programs such as NEXUS and Global Entry.[19] These programs have demonstrated that you can examine a person once through a rigorous application process, and on subsequent arrivals simply verify the identity of the person using an automated kiosk that reads the trav-

---

19   NEXUS and Global Entry are registered-traveler programs at US land borders in which frequent travelers can enroll by submitting information for criminal and terrorist background checks in exchange for expedited processing through security. "Global Entry is open to US citizens, lawful permanent residents, Dutch citizens, South Korean citizens and Mexican nationals." The NEXUS Program only applies to Canadian citizens and residents. See Global Entry Trusted Traveler Network, "Eligibility," www.globalentry.gov/eligibility.html.

eler's biometric data. The limitation of this approach, of course, is that it is a voluntary enrollment program. It is too expensive and too time consuming to attract occasional travelers and, by definition, screens people who present limited risk.

The third piece is the most interesting because it involves the key to transforming border management. Almost lost in all the talk about entry-exit controls is the insight that if you could ascertain and confirm the identity of all travelers prior to their crossing a border (and this only has to be done once because basic identity does not change, only behavior does), then you create a range of possibilities. Fixed identity opens the door to an approach based on movement, on patterns of behavior, and on anticipation. Entry decisions can be made in many different locations and in many different ways. For some travelers the entry decision may take place online; in fact, they may never need to see a border guard.

In 1994, Bill Gates made what was at the time a shrewd observation. He said that "banking is necessary, but banks are not." The truth of this statement is reflected in the rise of Amazon and iTunes and a whole new way of doing business. The same logic can also be applied to borders. A border is a place, but border management is an activity — that of making decisions. And, thanks to technology, decisions can be made in many places.

There are still many questions to work through, including issues related to privacy and the appetite of citizens to register their biometric information in order to cross borders. There will inevitably be references to Big Brother. But all such concerns need to be balanced against a growing recognition that our electronic world *already* threatens the security of our identities. Ultimately, the potential payoff for governments is easier and better security.

Works Cited

Anderson, Greg and Christopher Sands. 2007. *Negotiating North America: The Security and Prosperity Partnership.* Washington, DC: Hudson Institute. www.hudson.org/files/pdf_upload/HudsonNegotiatingNorthAmericaadvanceproof2.pdf.

Clarkson, Stephen. 2008. *Does North America Exist? Governing the Continent after NAFTA and 9/11.* Toronto: University of Toronto Press.

Council of the Americas. Undated. North American Competitiveness Council. www.as-coa.org/north-american-competitiveness-council.

Flynn Stephen E. and Jeane J. Kirkpatrick. 2004. Testimony of Commander, US Coast Guard (ret.), and Senior Fellow in National Security Studies at the Council on Foreign Relations, before the Senate Committee on Foreign Relations. *U.S.-Mexico: Immigration Policy & The Bilateral Relationship.* 108th Cong., 2d sess., March 23, 2004. www.aila.org/content/default.aspx?docid=10427.

Global Entry Trusted Traveler Network. Eligibility. Undated. www.globalentry.gov/eligibility.html.

Globerman, Steven and Paul Storer. 2008. *The Impacts of 9/11 on Canada-U.S. Trade.* Toronto: University of Toronto Press.

Government of Canada. 2005. Leaders' Statement: Security and Prosperity Partnership of North America Established. Statement delivered in Waco, Texas, March 23, 2005. www.spp-psp.gc.ca/eic/site/spp-psp.nsf/eng/00057.html.

Government of Canada and United States Government. 2001. Specifics of Secure and Smart Border Action Plan. http://georgewbush-whitehouse.archives.gov/news/releases/2002/01/20020107.html.

_____. 2001. U.S.-Canada Action Plan for Creating a Secure and Smart Border. http://georgewbush-whitehouse.archives.gov/news/releases/2002/01/20020107.html.

_____. 2011. Beyond the Border: A Shared Vision for Perimeter Security and Economic Competitiveness. www.dhs.gov/files/publications/beyond-the-border-action-plan.shtm.

Government of Mexico and United States Government. 2002. Specific Measures that Comprise Joint Action Plan with Mexico. http://georgewbush-whitehouse.archives.gov/infocus/usmxborder/01.html.

_____. 2002. U.S.-Mexico Border Partnership Action Plan. http://georgewbush-whitehouse.archives.gov/infocus/usmxborder/.

_____. 2004. Memorandum of Understanding on the Safe, Orderly, Dignified and Humane Repatriation of Mexican Nationals. www.ice.gov/doclib/foia/repatriation-agreements/memo-of-understanding-safe-orderly-dignified-humane-repatriation-of-mexican-nationals.pdf.

Mueller, John and Mark G. Stewart. 2011. *Terror, Security and Money: Balancing the Risks, Benefits, and Costs of Homeland Security.* Oxford: Oxford University Press.

Rosenblum, Marc R. 2011. *Obstacles and Opportunities for Regional Cooperation: The U.S.-Mexico Case*. Washington, DC: Migration Policy Institute. www.migrationpolicy.org/pubs/USMexico-cooperation.pdf.

Sands, Christopher. 2009. *Toward a New Frontier: Improving the U.S.-Canadian Border*. Washington, DC: Brookings Institution. www.brookings.edu/~/media/research/files/reports/2009/7/13%20canada%20sands/0713_canada_report.pdf.

_____. 2011. *The Canada Gambit: Will it Revive North America?* Washington, DC: Hudson Institute. www.hudson.org/files/publications/Canada%20Gambit%20Web.pdf.

US Department of Homeland Security. 2004. Fact Sheet: U.S.-Mexico Bilateral Meeting. News release, February 2, 2004. www.hsdl.org/?view&did=478530.

The White House. 2011. Declaration by President Obama and Prime Minister Harper of Canada - Beyond the Border. Press release, February 4, 2011. www.whitehouse.gov/the-press-office/2011/02/04/declaration-president-obama-and-prime-minister-harper-canada-beyond-bord.

_____. 2012. Joint Statement by North American Leaders. Press release, April 2, 2012. www.whitehouse.gov/the-press-office/2012/04/02/joint-statement-north-american-leaders.

CHAPTER 6

FALTERING SCHENGEN COOPERATION? THE CHALLENGES TO MAINTAINING A STABLE SYSTEM

Elizabeth Collett
Migration Policy Institute

I. Introduction

The Schengen area — a group of 26 European countries that have removed immigration and passport controls between their borders — is the result of a unique form of multilateral cooperation within the European Union (EU). It is admired globally for setting a new milestone in international collaboration on cross-border travel. For Europeans, the four-hour, high-speed train from Paris to Cologne or the six-and-a-half-hour train linking Munich, Vienna, and Budapest — unfettered by border guards — are tangible symbols of European integration, benefiting EU citizens and visitors alike. Despite these concrete advantages, however, the Schengen system has been severely strained over the past couple of years, starting with the particular migration flows precipitated by the Arab Spring in 2011. While the Schengen principles for border coordination continue to hold, they face extraordinary pressure, and both EU Member States and the European Commission are still some distance from finding a workable means of ensuring more stable cooperation in the future.

The pressures on the Schengen system can be broadly described as a confluence of toxic national politics, anxiety over exogenous geopolitical events (primarily in North Africa), and waning confidence in the ability of some EU Member States to live up to their commitments. But there is a growing sense of unease that long-term solutions for maintaining free movement through secure and equitable external border management may be impossible to forge, and that the project's architects will have to resign themselves to repairing rather than strengthening the Schengen system in the short to medium term.

This chapter explains some of the main drivers of tension, highlights the central challenges to finding a long-term solution for maintaining stable cooperation, and outlines the options available for continued collaboration within the Schengen framework. To this end, the chapter discusses the collective action needed from Member States to maintain the sharing of public goods.[1] Pressures on the Schengen system — and barriers to their resolution — can be seen through the lens of fluctuating and competing Member State interests. Collective action is not a new idea within the EU framework, and a number of analysts have highlighted the opportunities (and more frequently the problems) associated with maintaining shared action within the European Union, most commonly with respect to economic and monetary union, and the single market.[2] These ideas have also been applied in the area of Justice and Home Affairs (JHA), though less extensively.[3]

Put simply, the Schengen area is a shared public good. Its existence depends on Member States setting aside some sovereign rights and collaborating to ensure the internal security of the area. It is not a global public good, in that benefits of borderless travel are limited to participating states and individuals permitted to travel within the Schengen zone (EU and European Economic Area residents and Schengen visa holders). In exchange for this freedom of movement, Member States have agreed upon a number of compensatory mechanisms (e.g., external border management) and the development of critical elements of a Common European Asylum System (CEAS; e.g., the Dublin Regulation). These elements are not public goods in themselves — though they may benefit many, if not all, participants — but rather means to attaining the goal of an internally secure Schengen area.[4]

While Member States interests and benefits are broadly similar with respect to maintaining an area without internal borders, they diverge substantially with respect to the responsibilities each government has

---

1 Public goods are those which can be consumed by an individual, without affecting another individual's enjoyment of the same good. Classic examples include defense, or clean air.
2 See, for example, Stefan Collignon, "The Governance of European Public Goods," in *The EU Budget: What Should Go In? What Should Go Out?* ed. Daniel Tarschys (Stockholm: Swedish Institute for European Policy Studies, 2011), www.sieps.se/sites/default/files/2011_3.pdf.
3 See, for example, Claus-Jochen Haake, Tim Krieger, and Steffen Minter, "External Border Enforcement, Public Goods and Burden Sharing Mechanisms in the EU," in *Shaping the Normative Contours of the European Union: A Migration-Border Framework,* ed. Richard Zapato-Barrera (Barcelona: Barcelona Centre for International Affairs, 2010), www.cidob.org/en/publications/monographs/monographs/shaping_the_normative_contours_of_the_european_union_a_migration_border_framework; and Eiko Thielemann and Carolyn Armstrong, "Understanding European Asylum Cooperation under the Schengen/Dublin System: A Public Goods Framework," *European Security* 22, no. 2 (2013): 148–64.
4 Thielemann and Armstrong refer to these as intermediate public goods. See Thielemann and Armstrong, "Understanding European Asylum Cooperation."

been given to ensure that security is maintained. This is putting pressure on long-term sustainability of the Schengen system itself.

II. Background and State of Play

It is interesting to note that while Schengen is a flagship symbol of EU integration, it began outside the bounds of the EU framework. In 1985 five countries came together to negotiate and sign the founding Schengen cooperation agreement.[5] It took another ten years for the original agreement to become operational, and another two years for it to be brought within the fold of the European Union through the Amsterdam Treaty.[6] In the meantime, the European Free Trade Association (EFTA) states of Iceland, Lichtenstein, Norway, and Switzerland joined the initiative.[7]

Schengen cooperation has never been a smooth ride, and concerns over Member States' abilities to manage external borders and ports of entry have led to halts in cooperation and postponements of expansions and further agreements.[8] The accession of Romania and Bulgaria to the Schengen area has been repeatedly postponed over concerns about high levels of corruption and transnational crime. Separately, Schengen infrastructure has been hard to install: a planned upgrade of the common Schengen Information System (SIS), to include additional biometric data, is both over budget and overdue.[9]

In 2011, the Arab Spring became a major catalyst for Schengen reform. The geopolitical crisis put additional pressure on the Schengen system as large flows of migrants touched down on Maltese and Italian shores (mainly on the small island of Lampedusa). This sparked calls from the Maltese and Italian governments for pan-European support to help manage the inflows, specifically through financial and technical support and the relocation of refugees to other EU Member States. The calls for financial and technical support did not go unheeded: Frontex,

---

5   The Schengen Agreement of June 14, 1985, between the governments of the states of the Benelux Economic Union, the Federal Republic of Germany, and the French Republic, required the gradual abolition of checks at their common borders.
6   *Treaty of Amsterdam Amending the Treaty of the European Union, the Treaties Establishing the European Communities and Certain Related Acts*, November 10, 1997, EUR-Lex 340/1, http://eur-lex.europa.eu/en/treaties/dat/11997D/tif/JOC_1997_340__1_EN_0005.pdf.
7   At the time of writing, 22 European Union (EU) Member States participate. The United Kingdom and Ireland have opted out; and Bulgaria, Croatia, Cyprus, and Romania are obligated to join.
8   For example, Germany expressed concern about the quality of Austrian border controls in 1995, delaying Austria's accession to Schengen. As another example, there was an eight-month delay of expansion to Central European states in 2007 due to delays in implementing new common information systems.
9   Demetrios G. Papademetriou and Elizabeth Collett, *A New Architecture for Border Management*, (Washington, DC: Migration Policy Institute, 2011), www.migrationpolicy.org/pubs/borderarchitecture.pdf.

the EU border management agency, launched a joint operation in the area in late February 2011, and the European Commission made additional funding available.[10]

The calls for other Member States to relocate arrivals throughout the European Union, however, were met with silence. Some states highlighted that their annual asylum intake was already significant: during the second quarter of 2011, at the height of the crisis, both Germany and France received more asylum applications than Italy, while Sweden and the United Kingdom received only slightly fewer.[11] Other governments believed that Italy was not justified in asking for support because the country had closely collaborated with former Libyan ruler Muammar Gaddafi to prevent migrant inflows from the southern Mediterranean prior to revolution.

In the absence of any relocation mechanism, the Italian government offered residence permits to 22,000 Tunisian migrants — papers allowing them to move freely throughout Europe, which in turn led the French government reintroduced checks at its southern borders with Italy, particularly at the rail-lines. Seeking reconciliation, both heads of state met and drafted a joint letter to European Commission President José Manuel Barroso, including a request that Schengen rules be adjusted to allow states to close borders in "exceptional circumstances."[12]

Reintroduction of internal border controls is not without precedent. Member States may close internal borders for up to 30 days when there is a serious threat to public policy or national security, and this tack has been used when large sporting or political events might spark unrest.[13] Thus, the French-Italian request did not introduce a new concept into the Schengen agreement per se, but sought to expand — and possibly blur — the terms through which such controls may be reintroduced.

At the June 2011 European Summit, EU heads of state referred to Schengen as "one of the most tangible and successful achievements of European integration," affirming its status as a core European public

---

10 European Commission, "The European Commission's Response to the Migratory Flows from North Africa," (news release, April 8, 2011), http://europa.eu/rapid/press-release_MEMO-11-226_en.htm.
11 United Nations High Commissioner for Refugees (UNHCR), *Asylum Levels and Trends in Industrialized Countries* (Geneva: UNHCR, 2011), www.unhcr.org/4fdf1b779.html.
12 Joint letter from Nicolas Sarkozy, President of the Republic of France, and Silvio Berlusconi, Prime Minister of Italy, to Herman Van Rompuy, President of the European Council, and José Manuel Barroso, President of the European Commission, April 26, 2011, Rome, www.ambafrance-uk.org/Letter-from-French-and-Italian.
13 Indeed, on more than one occasion, border controls have been reintroduced over concerns related to immigration and asylum. For example, the Belgian government reintroduced border controls in 2001, citing a risk of increased asylum applications, following a decision one year earlier to reintroduce controls during a regularization process.

good.[14] However, a number of Member States have continued to question the future functioning of the Schengen system, citing the need for revised mechanisms to reduce the risks of weak external borders and to increase internal surveillance. In Denmark there was a short-lived effort to re-establish customs checks along Danish borders with Germany and Sweden, ostensibly to address transborder crime, but in reality responding to populist political pressure.[15] The Netherlands has installed security cameras in the border stretches of national highways in a bid to stop and find unauthorized travelers and criminals.[16]

In 2012 the debate moved to finding institutional solutions at the EU level. The European Commission outlined a series of reforms to Schengen to prevent a repeat of the spring 2011 events.[17] In particular, the Commission proposed:

- A "mechanism" to respond to exceptional pressures and guidelines, outlining the circumstances under which Member States may legitimately introduce internal border controls.

- A reinforced evaluation mechanism to ensure that all border agencies are compliant in their implementation of the Schengen border code. Critically, the Commission proposed taking over the process, no longer trusting the current peer-review process managed by Member States.

- A concrete articulation of circumstances under which a Member State might be shut out from the Schengen system for "persistent failure to adequately protect a part of the EU's external border." This clause is aimed squarely at Greece, and suggests that failure to bolster the Greek-Turkish border could result in Greece being pushed out of the Schengen system until border controls are deemed sufficiently adequate.

The Commission's proposal highlights that external events leading to a sudden influx of third-country nationals without authorization could provide just cause for the reintroduction of border controls. The key question remains who will have the authority to decide when, where, and for how long the controls remain in place. The idea that this should be in the Commission's hands drew strong opposition from Member

---

14 European Council, "Conclusions: 23/24 June 2011," EUCO 23/11, Brussels, June 24, 2011, http://ec.europa.eu/commission_2010-2014/president/news/speeches-statements/pdf/20110624_1_en.pdf.
15 The new government removed these controls following national elections in September 2011, and pressure from both the European Commission and neighboring Member States.
16 Dutch Ministry of the Interior, "Factsheet Gebruik @migoboras," February 9, 2012, The Hague, www.rijksoverheid.nl/bestanden/documenten-en-publicaties/brochures/2012/02/09/factsheet-gebruik-migoboras/20120127-factsheet-migo-boras.pdf.
17 European Commission, "Schengen Governance — Strengthening the Area without Internal Border Control," COM [2011] 561, Brussels, September 16, 2011, http://eur-lex.europa.eu/LexUriServ/LexUriServ.do?uri=COM:2011:0561:FIN:EN:PDF.

States, not least France, Germany, and Spain.[18] The European Parliament also wished to have a say in regulatory developments, and voted to suspend cooperation with the Justice and Home Affairs Council after the Danish EU Presidency shut it out of negotiations.[19]

One year later, the Commission, Council, and European Parliament agreed on a compromise.[20] The new evaluation mechanism remains broadly as listed above, though the European Commission and Member States have joint responsibility for Schengen evaluation. This falls short of the Commission's bid for sole responsibility, but is an improvement on its original status as merely an observer. In addition, the Commission is now in the lead regarding the development of evaluation priorities and reporting, also relying on risk assessments from Frontex.

The EU institutions have also agreed upon an amendment to the Schengen Border Code, which introduces the possibility of closing internal borders should serious deficiencies regarding the management of external borders be found. Critically, the rules state that this is a measure of last resort, and must be based on a European Commission report, not at the initiative of Member States themselves.

These new rules only address a superficial challenge: reducing the ability of a single Member State to 1) renege on external border management commitments, and 2) spontaneously close internal borders as a result of perceived mismanagement elsewhere. However, as this chapter shows, these rules merely obscure a series of deeper issues and tensions that are unlikely to recede in the medium to long term.

III. Drivers of Tension

EU policy is not formulated in isolation. The situation at Europe's borders, and the politics both between and within EU Member States, can all have a significant effect on Schengen cooperation by affecting Member States' interests and the relative costs of their participation. Looking beyond the current impasse, one can see that the underlying drivers of tension — including foreign policy, national politics, and intra-EU politics — are unlikely to decrease over the months and years

---

18 German Federal Ministry of the Interior, "Joint press statement by the interior ministers of France, Germany and Spain on the Commission's proposals for strengthening Schengen governance," (news release, September 13, 2011), www.bmi.bund.de/SharedDocs/Pressemitteilungen/EN/2011/09/schengen.html?nr=109632.
19 European Parliament, "EP suspends cooperation with Council following decision on Schengen area rules," June 13, 2012, www.europarl.europa.eu/news/en/headlines/content/20120613STO46764/html/EP-suspends-cooperation-with-Council-following-decision-on-Schengen-area-rules.
20 European Council, "Council and the European Parliament reach a provisional agreement on the Schengen Governance legislative package," (press release 221, May 30, 2013), www.consilium.europa.eu/uedocs/cms_data/docs/pressdata/en/jha/137348.pdf.

ahead. As a result, Member States' interest in Schengen cooperation is likely to fluctuate in coming years, contributing to its instability.

A. Foreign Policy

Geopolitical upheaval, specifically in North Africa, catalyzed the most recent crisis. While the numbers arriving in Europe were modest compared to those arriving in contiguous African countries, the debate was not driven by the *actual* number of migrants arriving at Europe's borders but rather by the potential number that might follow. In Italy, for example, politicians predicted 200,000-300,000 arrivals, that would bring Italy "to its knees," a characterization encouraged by beleaguered Libyan dictator Qaddafi.[21] While the situation in North Africa has calmed, the crisis in Syria — and a wave of humanitarian migration to neighboring states, including Turkey — still looms large with more than 2 million refugees by September 2013.[22]

Less visible, but no less serious, have been the political debates surrounding visa liberalization — the practice of lifting the requirement for certain third-country nationals to obtain a Schengen visa before travelling to the EU Schengen space — particularly with European Neighborhood countries.[23] Over the past four years, the European Union has liberalized visa policies with most of the Balkan countries — Macedonia, Montenegro, and Serbia in July 2009; and Albania and Bosnia and Herzegovina in November 2010 — though not without controversy. Liberalization was followed by high numbers of Balkan nationals claiming asylum in EU Member States, notably Belgium, the Netherlands, Sweden, and Germany. As a result, the European Commission and EU Member States are now considering a "safeguard" mechanism for reintroducing visa controls should asylum claims rise substantially.

Exogenous events in themselves are not capable of sinking the Schengen system; however, they expose underlying weaknesses and inflame pre-existing tensions, particularly when those events affect some Member States disproportionately. The troubled efforts to resolve the most recent crisis suggests the European Union is not ready to handle the inflow of migrants after a Syrian government collapse, short of expelling Greece from the Schengen system and passing the problem on to Turkey, Jordan, and Lebanon. It is unclear whether the new Schengen rules will be sufficient to prevent future cooperative breakdown.

---

21 Philippe Fargues and Christine Fandrich, *Migration after the Arab Spring* (Florence: Migration Policy Centre, 2012), www.migrationpolicycentre.eu/docs/MPC 2012 EN 09.pdf.
22 UNHCR, "Number of Syrian refugees tops 2 million mark with more on the way," (press release, September 3, 2013), www.unhcr.org/522495669.html.
23 The European Neighborhood Policy (ENP), developed in 2004, aims to transform relations between the European Union and 16 of its closest neighbors: Algeria, Armenia, Azerbaijan, Belarus, Egypt, Georgia, Israel, Jordan, Lebanon, Libya, Moldova, Morocco, the Occupied Palestinian Territory, Syria, Tunisia, and the Ukraine.

B. National Politics

The 2011 Schengen crisis was not only a crisis of EU cooperation, but a reflection of increasingly tense national political debates on immigration across Europe, as governments play out their national politics on the EU stage. A key political reality in many countries is that small yet powerful minorities are sometimes capable of dictating immigration outcomes. The Italian and French government actions during 2011 were shaped by domestic political pressures (from the right-wing political parties Lega Nord in Italy and National Front in France) to be tough on immigration from third countries. In Denmark, the government moved to restore customs controls at Danish borders in response to calls from the Danish People's Party, a right-wing party that advocates immigration restrictions.

In the immigration, asylum, and free movement policy portfolios, the level of solidarity necessary for EU cooperation requires that countries set aside a certain amount of national sovereignty. In reality, immigration policy in Europe never strays far from the constraints of domestic politics. Populist pressure means that EU Member States are finding it harder and harder to collaborate. It is difficult to distinguish between policymakers' legitimate national policy concerns and the tendency to cater to domestic electoral interests as they advocate for changes in EU policy. Former French President Nicolas Sarkozy's election speeches centered on the need to "reconsider" Schengen — and even included threats to withdraw France from the system altogether[24] — creating a stark contrast with his reputation as a committed "Europeanist."

Tinkering with Schengen may not necessarily be a long-term vote-winning policy for national politicians. During the October 2011 national elections in Denmark, the popularity of the Danish People's Party declined significantly, and the new socialist government announced that it would abandon the policy of reestablishing internal border controls. This may suggest that despite the short-term benefits of populist political stances, attempts to look tough may be ultimately self-defeating. Nonetheless, they have a destabilizing effect on the Schengen system by making Member States less confident about the gains from cooperation.

C. Intra-EU Politics

The institutions of the European Union often find themselves with differing priorities. Additionally, EU Member States do not act in a vacuum once away from the negotiating table. The relevance of small regional or issue-focused blocs, and the enduring competition between Member States for (on the one hand) the most talented and skilled international workers but (on the other) the lowest numbers of asylum seekers, creates a multitude of alliances and rivalries that complicate cooperation.

---

24 Nikolaj Nielsen, "Sarkozy Threatens to End EU Passport-Free Travel," *EUobserver*, March 12, 2012, http://euobserver.com/9/115556.

Three main groups emerge. First, there are states in the north of Europe that are primarily concerned by the knock-on effects of Schengen travel, such as secondary movements and numbers of asylum seekers. This group includes Austria, Belgium, Denmark, France, Germany, the Netherlands, Sweden, and to some extent the United Kingdom (though it is not part of the Schengen system itself).[25] These countries see themselves as the responsible guarantors of Europe's external borders, willing to donate financial and human resources but intolerant of substandard border management. Indeed, Northern states are some of the most frequent participants in joint border operations in the Mediterranean, donating personnel and equipment to support those operations.[26]

Second, there are the states with the greatest direct external-border management responsibility because they are on the Mediterranean coast and/or share land borders with potential sending countries. The most formally organized are those of the Quadro group, consisting of Cyprus, Greece, Italy, and Malta. Other external border countries, not least Poland and Spain, have similar concerns. These countries see themselves as beleaguered nations taking on the burden of border management on behalf of northern countries.

Third, there are those countries seen by others as failing in their obligations to the promise of Schengen. These include Greece and Italy, and potentially Bulgaria and Romania should they be given Schengen status. These countries are willing to resort to unilateral actions — from building walls along the border, to bilateral return agreements with Libya — in order to fulfill their obligations.

These groups come together to argue for different solutions within the Schengen system, not all of which are mutually compatible, and many of which are based on deeply held principles. However, these alliances are not fixed; they fluctuate according to context. Italy and Malta may find common cause when discussing border management with northern states, but fiercely battle each other over whether boats should land in Lampedusa or Malta. Such shifting alliances make it difficult for EU institutions to negotiate an equitable solution that can satisfy all national preferences. Meanwhile, each national political debate focuses narrowly on the "winners and losers" of intra-EU collaboration, further weakening the spirit of compromise upon which Schengen is predicated.

---

25   Many of these countries co-authored an informal paper to the Justice and Human Affairs Council meeting in March. See Council of the European Union, "Common responses to current challenges by Member States most affected by secondary mixed migration flows," 7431/12, Brussels, March 9, 2012, www.statewatch.org/news/2012/mar/eu-council-secondary-migration-flows-7431-12.pdf.

26   See the list of joint operations, which can be found on the Frontex website: Frontex, "Archive of Joint Operations," www.frontex.europa.eu/operations/types-of-operations/general.

Pressure points for entry to Europe have shifted between the southern and eastern borders over the past decade. It is clear that some countries bear the brunt (real or perceived) of reducing irregular border crossings: first Spain, then Malta and Italy, and more recently Greece. The perception among these countries that they have been "burdened" by external border management, and northern countries have avoided taking their fair share of responsibility, is enduring and has yet to be sustainably resolved. Northern states — such as Germany, Netherlands, France, and the United Kingdom — note that they deal with more spontaneous asylum applications than their southern partners, and believe that offering financial and technical support is sufficient. Southern states would like to establish deeper cooperation, including a system for the relocation of refugees (and possibly asylum seekers) across the European Union.

The broader challenge that such entrenched regional factions pose is that they are based on a mutual perception that it is the "other" that is failing in its obligations. For northern countries, southern (and to a lesser extent, eastern) countries are failing to meet their Schengen commitments and risking the project, while passing on the costs of absorbing or deporting the asylum seekers and unauthorized migrants who then move north through the Schengen area. In the Netherlands, for example, internal border surveillance (legitimately conducted under Schengen rules) revealed 1,733 unauthorized migrants alongside other individuals involved in cross-border crime in 2012.[27] From the perspective of southern states, the north is complacently enjoying the benefits of Schengen without contributing adequately toward its overall costs. One of Frontex's early missions off the coast of Malta, Nautilus, had to be abandoned in 2007 in part due to a lack of contributions such as patrol boats and technical assistance from other Member States.[28] Both claims would seem to be empirically sound, yet each group refutes the importance of the counter-claim. This is the crux of the 'burden-sharing' conundrum.

IV. Bolstering the Schengen System

It is important to remember that the Schengen system is, in some ways, ahead of its time. It is certainly more developed than other forms of EU cooperation, and it goes beyond the current level of convergence on immigration and asylum policies among the 28 EU Member States. As a result, it is easy to forget that within the bigger picture of EU integration, Schengen is particularly fragile, dependent as it is on the success and/or failure of cooperation and mutual understanding between

---

27 Andrew Rettman, "Criminals Exploiting EU Travel Freedoms, Dutch Data Shows," *EUobserver*, March 15, 2013, http://euobserver.com/justice/119440.
28 Derek Lutterbeck, "Small Frontier Island: Malta and the Challenge of Irregular Immigration," *Mediterranean Quarterly* 20, no. 1 (2009): 119–44.

European countries. There are a number of ways in which the effects of current tensions might be diminished. However, for various reasons — mostly concerning national and regional-level politics — these solutions seem distant.

A. Completing the EU Immigration Project

As noted above, sustainable and stable Schengen cooperation relies on a number of other interdependent EU projects. The Schengen Agreement explicitly identified external border control as a counterbalance to internal border deconstruction, but the system also relies on effective cooperation in the areas of asylum and irregular migration, and a consensus with respect to legal immigration policy. If mutual understanding between EU institutions and Member States — or among Member States themselves — breaks down in any one of these areas, Schengen comes under pressure. If Schengen comes under pressure, so do other forms of external cooperation, such as visa liberalization, a Neighbourhood Policy initiative dependent on the ability to issue visas that cover the entire Schengen area.

1. Border Management

The survival of the Schengen area depends on the existence of a strong external border and the shared responsibility among all Member States to maintain it. Thus, all Member States must be comfortable with the quality of border control *and* the equitable contributions of those responsible. The fact that each country remains responsible for its own border management means that a great deal of trust among countries is required. While such trust has come under pressure during moments of enlargement and crisis, it has ultimately been maintained.

The mutual, entrenched perception that border management failures are due to the behavior of *other* Member States has had a deleterious effect on the trust that underlies Schengen. In the absence of an equitable and sustainable compromise, this trust will continue to erode until one external-border country is unable — or unwilling — to live up to its obligations to secure its borders. The Italian action to allow Tunisian arrivals to travel on through Europe can, in some ways, be read as a warning shot to EU partners.

What solutions exist? The proposed Schengen reform (see above) provides a negative one: should a Member State not live up to its border obligations, then it may face temporary expulsion from the Schengen space.

Beyond this, the European Union has focused on bolstering the response capacity of Frontex as a way to reduce inequity. But as many commentators — from the European Parliament to Human

Rights Watch — have noted, Frontex is merely a coordinator.[29] It lacks accountability and autonomy as an agency and must, at last resort, rely on Member States for its authority. It also relies on Member States for expertise; the Rapid Border Intervention Teams (RABIT)[30] deployed to the Greek-Turkish border in 2010 comprised 175 officials from a pool of Member States and other Schengen-associated countries, overseen by Greek authorities.[31] Thus, Frontex is at best a stopgap to ameliorate the burden on Member States with vulnerable external borders, rather than a system of rebalancing.

In the long term, any mechanism for reintroducing border controls will have to be accompanied by a substantive set of burden-sharing measures, capable of satisfying states both in the south and north. However, beyond the response described above, states have struggled to collectively articulate what this might mean. Long-term success may lie in the completion of other projects, such as the Common European Asylum System (CEAS).

2. Common European Asylum System

The challenge to Schengen posed by the unfinished CEAS revolves around the secondary movement — from the first country of arrival across Europe to other countries — of asylum seekers and refugees following their arrival in Europe. Problems of such secondary movement are, in turn, exacerbated by enduring differences in how nations across the EU-28 address these migrants.

The cornerstone of the CEAS — and the most necessary element to ensure continued Member State collaboration — is the Dublin Regulation, which states that asylum seekers should be returned to the first EU country they entered. This is apparently necessary to ensure that asylum seekers do not "shop" around the EU for their preferred destination, taking advantage of the lack of internal borders. The agreement is based on the erroneous premise that there would be no difference in protection and procedural standards across the European Union. Subsequent EU legislation — the Directives on Reception Conditions,

---

29 See for example, Human Rights Watch, *The EU's Dirty Hands: Frontex Involvement in Ill-Treatment of Migrant Detainees in Greece* (New York: Human Rights Watch, 2011), www.hrw.org/sites/default/files/reports/greece0911webwcover_0.pdf; and European Parliament, Policy Department C: Citizens' Rights and Constitutional Affairs, *Implementation of the EU Charter of Fundamental Rights and its Impact on EU Home Affairs Agencies: Frontex, Europol and the European Asylum Support Office* (Brussels: European Parliament, 2011), www.ceps.eu/ceps/dld/6312/pdf.

30 The idea behind Frontex's Rapid Border Intervention Teams (RABIT) is to be able respond to cases of urgent and exceptional migratory pressure with rapid deployment of border guards on a European level. The teams are intended to provide short-term assistance, and the responsibility for the control and surveillance of the external borders remains with the Member States. See Frontex, *RABIT Operation 2010 Evaluation Report* (Warsaw: Frontex, 2011), www.frontex.europa.eu/assets/Attachments_News/fer_rabit_2010_screen_v6.pdf.

31 Frontex, "Frontex to Deploy 175 Specialist Border Personnel to Greece,"(press release, October 29, 2010), www.frontex.europa.eu/news/frontex-to-deploy-175-specialist-border-personnel-to-greece-9neidF.

Procedures, and Qualification — were then expected to transform the premise into reality. There remains strong evidence that asylum determinations in each country still vary significantly, and that the treatment of asylum seekers is often substandard. The European Council for Refugees and Exiles (ECRE) has highlighted that, in 2010, the number of positive decisions on asylum applications varied from 3 percent in Greece to 100 percent in Portugal, with the other Member States covering the entire spectrum in between. Differences for asylum seekers of the same nationality are also stark: an Iraqi national had a 10 percent chance of recognition in Greece in 2010, compared to a 78 percent chance of acquiring refugee status in Belgium.[32]

The endurance of the Dublin Regulation in the face of such inconsistency (it has now been renegotiated for the third time) highlights the lynchpin status of this particular piece of legislation: without it, not only would common asylum rules be in jeopardy, but external border management and — subsequently — Schengen cooperation might crumble. Meanwhile, national implementation of EU asylum legislation — meant to ensure a basic standard of protection across the European Union — remains patchy. In January 2011 the European Court of Human Rights ruled that to return asylum seekers to Greece would amount to inhumane and degrading treatment, contrary to the European Convention on Human Rights.[33] Following this ruling, a number of European governments (including Belgium, Germany, and Sweden) suspended returns to Greece.

Since then, there has been surprisingly little focus on addressing the conditions of detention for asylum seekers and others in Greece, despite documented evidence of extremely poor conditions.[34] (This is in contrast to other strategies for managing the migrants who arrive in Europe through Greece: e.g. Frontex, with the support of Member States, quickly formed a RABIT team to bolster the Greek-Turkish border). This reveals an inherent skew in the ability of EU institutions and their stakeholders to respond to issues that only indirectly affect their own situation. The knock-on effects of poor border management are immediately visible. However, the effects of substandard detention conditions, or poor decision-making, are only brought to light by a judicial decision.

In this context, the long-term goal of completing a functioning and equitable CEAS seems a distant one. There is little imperative for Member States, comfortable with the functioning of their own systems,

---

32 See the European Council on Refugees and Exiles (ECRE) website for a visual representation of these disparities, based on UNHCR Global Trend data. ECRE, "Asylum Lottery in the EU in 2010," http://ecre.org/component/content/article/56-ecre-actions/246-asylum-lottery-in-the-eu-in-2010.html.
33 European Court of Human Rights, "Case of M.S.S. vs. Belgium and Greece: Judgment," Strasbourg, January 21, 2011, http://hudoc.echr.coe.int/sites/eng/pages/search.aspx?i=001-103050.
34 Human Rights Watch, The EU's Dirty Hands.

to prioritize further collaboration. For some countries, the current legislation (recently re-tweaked to address glaring issues), bolstered by the introduction of operational support through the European Asylum Support Office (EASO), is more than sufficiently "common" or uniform. However, even with EASO asylum officers to help states with less capacity process asylum claimants, the deficiencies highlighted above are likely to persist, not least the wide variance in decision-making on applications for asylum.

What long-term options exist for the CEAS? Some countries, such as the United Kingdom in 2003, have suggested that common processing centers may assist with EU asylum harmonization,[35] while others have highlighted the need for a full-fledged relocation system for asylum seekers within Europe. Both options have significant pitfalls. Common processing centers, whether internally or externally located, raise both practical and legal issues around which country retains practical and jurisdictional responsibility for processing, ensuring adequate levels of protection, and dealing with applicants whose claims are not recognized.[36] Certainly, Australia's experience with the extraterritorial processing center on the island of Nauru highlights the challenges for just one jurisdiction;[37] the level of collaboration needed to maintain EU-wide processing centers suggests this is politically unfeasible as well as legally and practically complex. Relocation systems, in turn, depend upon finding equitable and practical criteria for determining how asylum seekers might be distributed throughout the European Union. Within a single country, redistribution mechanisms have sometimes proved controversial, and any mechanism based on population, economic growth, and pre-existing numbers of refugees will be difficult to negotiate.[38]

At the current time, there are few plans for the future development of CEAS, and none that seem particularly advantageous or practicable. Following the completion of the renegotiation of the key asylum Directives in Spring 2013, it is clear that there is a high level of political fatigue. Next steps, if any, would have to be incremental, and the most stable, long-term solution — completely harmonized decision-making and appeals systems — remains the *least* politically and practicably feasible.

---

35 Letter from British Prime Minister Tony Blair to Greek Prime Minister Costas Simitis, March 10, 2003, www.statewatch.org/news/2003/apr/blair-simitis-asile.pdf.
36 Council of Europe, Parliamentary Assembly Committee on Migration, Refugees and Population, "Assessment of Transit and Processing Centres as a Response to Mixed Flows of Migrants and Asylum Seekers," June 13, 2007,http://assembly.coe.int/ASP/Doc/XrefViewHTML.asp?FileID=11557&Language=EN.
37 See, for example, Christopher D. Foulkes, "Australia's Boat People: Asylum Challenges and Two Decades of Policy Experimentation," *Migration Information Source,* July 2012, http://migrationinformation.org/Feature/display.cfm?ID=899.
38 European Commission, *Study on the Feasibility of Establishing a Mechanism for Relocation of the Beneficiaries of International Protection* (Copenhagen: Ramboll Management Consulting and Eurasylum Limited, 2010), http://ec.europa.eu/home-affairs/doc_centre/asylum/docs/final_report_relocation_of_refugees.pdf.

The interdependence of all these systems — Schengen, border management, and CEAS — and their continued incompleteness, means that significant achievement or crisis in one system will continue to have ripple effects across all EU immigration and asylum management systems. However, to resolve this situation decisively — either by harmonizing immigration and asylum laws *or* by dismantling Schengen — is not in any Member State's interest. Instead, the Commission will have to continue to make compromise decisions, and find ways to circumvent and manage these conflicts. Meanwhile, any shock to one system will have a domino effect across all.

B. National Policy Convergence

EU-wide legislative cooperation has been difficult to come by in the areas of immigration (legal migration in particular) and asylum. Implementation of existing EU law is still patchy, and Member States demonstrate little interest in collaborating more deeply in this policy area. However, over the last couple of years, there have been several indications that, in the *absence* of completely harmonized third-country immigration policies, the conflict between internal systems of free movement and diverging national policies is placing adverse pressure on trust and cooperation within the Schengen system. While there may be little political will to move forward, maintaining the "halfway house" status quo will be unsustainable in the long term.

The French-Italian dispute at the internal border highlighted one essential fact: that immigration policy decisions adopted by a single Member State may have unwanted spillover effects for other (particularly neighboring) Member States. This is not the first occasion that unilateral policy decisions have affected EU cooperation on immigration. The 2006 Spanish decision to regularize around 600,000 irregular migrants upset the French government, as officials there believed many of those offered legal status would then travel to France.[39] Real or imagined, this concern sparked a debate on regularization at the EU level resulting first in a "mutual information mechanism" (whereby governments were asked to inform fellow states of impending amnesties), and eventually in a political statement in the European Pact on Immigration and Asylum, promulgated by the French EU presidency in 2008.[40]

This debate highlighted how trust among Member States is predicated on an unspoken set of parameters — the common belief that these states all hold roughly the same philosophies and priorities — within which governments make national choices. The EU Immigration Pact was an effort to articulate these priorities.

---

39 BBC News, "France Urges EU Immigration Curbs," September 29, 2006, http://news.bbc.co.uk/2/hi/europe/5391920.stm.
40 European Council, "Council Decision of 5 October 2006 on the Establishment of a Mutual Information Mechanism Concerning Member States' Measures in the Areas of Asylum and Immigration, 2006/688/EC" October 5, 2006, http://eur-lex.europa.eu/LexUriServ/LexUriServ.do?uri=CELEX:32006D0688:EN:NOT.

Beyond formal policy changes, discretionary decision-making may also stress the Schengen system. It has become clear that different Member States interpret and apply EU rules very differently. For example, levels of returns of irregular migrants vary significantly from country to country.[41] Similarly, research on the issuance of Schengen visas in the Ukraine highlights that processes vary — indeed, the visa refusal rate ranges from 2 percent for Slovakia to over 10 percent for Germany[42] — and applicants know which consulates and countries might offer the quickest and most favorable route into the European Union. Finally, citizenship policy — such as the Hungarian policy to extend citizenship rights to all ethnic Hungarians — means that a large number of non-EU nationals have acquired EU citizenship without ever having resided within the European Union.[43]

All of these discrepancies place low-level pressure on the system as a whole. While harmonized legal immigration policies seem ever more distant a reality, EU Member States and institutions need to find some way to ensure sufficient common ground for national policy choices and consistent implementation of common EU policies. However, even a cursory glance at the lengthy, piecemeal negotiations to develop common policy on seasonal workers and intra-corporate transferees in recent years, and the low common standards created through EU legislation for family reunification, long-term residence, and third-country national workers, suggest that convergence is a long way off. National needs and interests remain starkly different — further exacerbated by economic crisis — and governments are intent on retaining as much control over immigration policies as possible.

C. Thickening Institutional Cooperation

Despite the strong desire to retain control over Schengen, the reality is that new actors are likely to dilute national autonomy, and by association, interfere with national interests. Just as a larger number of committees, task forces, and working groups are needed to track JHA developments within the Council and the Commission, thus spreading the locus of knowledge and responsibility, so new actors are flexing their decision-making muscles.

Most significantly, the European Parliament now has a say in the Schengen debate; as one might expect, it takes a more pro-EU institutional position, which is intended to reflect its role as the direct representa-

---

41 See, for example, European Commission, "Communication on Migration," Brussels, COM(2011)248, May 4, 2011, http://ec.europa.eu/home-affairs/news/intro/docs/1_EN_ACT_part1_v11.pdf.
42 Iryna Sushko et al., *Schengen Consulates in Assessments and Ratings. Visa Practices of the EU Member States in Ukraine* (Kiev: Europe without Barriers, 2010), http://novisa.com.ua/upload/file/Viza_Monitor_ENG-3.pdf.
43 Irina Molodikova, "Patterns of East to West Migration in the Context of European Migration Systems: Possibilities and Limits of Migration Control," *Demográfia* 51, no. 5 (2008) English Edition: 5–35.

tive of EU citizens, though public skepticism of the European Union is rising across the continent. In November 2011, the Parliament's Committee on Civil Liberties, Justice, and Home Affairs (LIBE) endorsed a report stating that the Commission should have more say in evaluating Schengen and the mechanism to reintroduce internal border controls.[44] While the European Parliament can be circumvented through changing the legal basis of the Schengen evaluation rules (as the Danish Presidency did in June 2012), the collateral damage is significant.[45]

Second, the judicial system is likely to get more involved in issues pertaining to JHA, in the shape of both the European Court of Justice and the European Court of Human Rights. The most recent ruling from the latter court *(Hirsi Jamaa and Others v. Italy)* determined that the interception and return (refoulement) of boatloads of migrants en route from Libya without consideration of their potential asylum claim, under the terms of a bilateral agreement with Libya, was illegal. This activism highlights that Member States alone cannot determine the rules of external border cooperation, which is in turn needed to maintain a resilient Schengen system. The European Commission is also aware that cases of non-implementation of Schengen rules, or a unilateral decision to close borders, might also be taken to the European Court of Justice in the future. Decisions taken by Member States today may well be overturned by court rulings tomorrow.

Third, the need for effective management of complex, half-finished systems such as Schengen, CEAS, and external borders management has led to the creation of a number of EU agencies, notably Frontex and the European Asylum Support Office, but also a new information technology agency to manage JHA information systems.

Member States have welcomed, indeed encouraged, the development of agencies to foster operational cooperation, which in turn helps individual administrations sidestep some of the more tricky aspects of border and asylum cooperation. (Frontex's coordinating role was further strengthened in late 2011). Meanwhile, two points are clear: first, as these agencies mature, it will become ever harder for Member States to maintain their autonomous stance on border and asylum system management; second, the quasi-operational status of these agencies highlights that sustainable cooperation can only be maintained in the long term with greater harmonization among Member States.

---

44 European Parliament, Committee on Civil Liberties, Justice, and Home Affairs (LIBE), *Draft Report on the Proposal for a Regulation of the European Parliament and of the Council on the Establishment of an Evaluation Mechanism to Verify Application of the Schengen Acquis* (Brussels: European Parliament, 2011), www.europarl.europa.eu/meetdocs/2009_2014/documents/libe/pr/860/860326/860326en.pdf; European Parliament, "Schengen: stricter EU rules to prevent illegal border checks," (news release, November 29, 2011), www.europarl.europa.eu/news/en/pressroom/content/20111129IPR32707/html/Schengen-stricter-EU-rules-to-prevent-illegal-border-checks.

45 As noted above, the LIBE Committee boycotted discussion of a series of JHA measures in protest at being locked out of negotiations.

Thickening institutional cooperation can minimize the impact of national policy choices within the Schengen system, as oversight becomes more pronounced. However, this promises to be a long-term endeavor unlikely to bear significant fruit for some years to come.

By contrast, the long-held hope that the Lisbon Treaty would smooth the progress of EU common immigration policies by giving the European Commission a stronger role in their development has not been fulfilled. Instead, there has been something of a chilling effect. Member States seem more reluctant than ever to cede sovereignty upward — even when it may be in their long-term interest — and are content with a quasi-intergovernmental approach, even if less efficient. This is reflected in the final Schengen Evaluation Mechanism agreement, which allows for the temporary reintroduction of internal borders under extreme circumstances. France and Italy asked for the mechanism, subsequently endorsed by the European Council. And while a majority of Member States agreed that an EU-level safeguard was necessary, they were united in their opposition to the idea of the European Commission arbitrating the safeguard — a rare show of cooperation.[46]

It seems unlikely that an EU-level safeguard managed by Member States in conjunction with other EU institutions would function effectively, and more important, survive politically. A review of the various committees that have overseen the development of the second-generation Schengen Information System suggests a Kafkaesque warren of working groups with little centralized knowledge or, critically, responsibility.[47] However, such is their concern about devolving power to the Commission that Member States are willing to introduce a *weak* safeguard to retain *strong* autonomy. That Member States find this trade-off acceptable, rather than self-defeating, is at the heart of the challenge to future Schengen cooperation.

V. Broader Interests at Stake

Given all the challenges outlined above, it seems unlikely that the balance of interests among Member States, and the balance of power

---

[46] Council of the European Union, "Amended Proposal for a Regulation of the European Parliament and of the Council on the Establishment of an Evaluation and Monitoring Mechanism to Verify the Application of the Schengen Acquis," Brussels, June 4, 2012, http://register.consilium.europa.eu/pdf/en/12/st05/st05754-re06.en12.pdf; European Commission, "Proposal for a Regulation of the European Parliament and of the Council Amending Regulation (EC) No 562/2006 in Order to Provide for Common Rules on the Temporary Reintroduction of Border Control at Internal Borders in Exceptional Circumstances," Brussels, December 9, 2011, http://ec.europa.eu/dgs/home-affairs/e-library/docs/pdf/560_en_en.pdf.

[47] For a schematic of the EU governance framework, see Joanna Parkin, *The Difficult Road to the Schengen Information System II: The Legacy of 'Laboratories' and the Cost for Fundamental Rights and the Rule of Law* (Brussels: Centre for European Policy Studies, 2011): 19, www.ceps.eu/ceps/dld/4373/pdf.

among institutions, will soon achieve the equilibrium that would best bolster the Schengen system and secure its future. But the Member States may have too quickly absorbed (and dismissed) the significant benefits that Schengen has bestowed, focusing instead on the more immediate problems and additional costs. It is thus worth reflecting on the broader set of interests at stake, which indicate that abandoning Schengen is neither politically palatable nor practically possible.

A. *The Benefits of Schengen*

First and foremost, the Schengen area offers Europeans huge advantages by facilitating mobility, tourism, and trade — all key benefits in an increasingly competitive global economy. For example, tourism directly or indirectly accounts for about 10 percent of the EU economy and employs 9.7 million EU citizens.[48] As the leading tourist destination in the world, Europe's economic interests are well-served by facilitating tourist travel.

The information systems that facilitate Schengen cooperation (such as the Schengen Information System and the Visa Information System) have arguably improved European security overall, by identifying fake or stolen documents, or those who have a criminal history. Additionally, EU Member States are keen to see additional systems, such as a European Surveillance System (EUROSUR) and an entry-exit system, put in place. Some unresolved issues are the extent to which security may come at the expense of liberal goals regarding individual rights, as well as concerns about data collection and privacy.[49]

Schengen is also a source of pride for Europeans, both internally and on the international stage. It is the envy of other regional cooperation arrangements, the Association of Southeast Asian Nations (ASEAN) among them; most regional cooperation arrangements now include free movement as an aspiration. Schengen is one of the most visible successes of the EU project.

Finally, it has structural advantages for the European Union's external relations, not least within the European Neighborhood area, as Schengen can be used to influence third countries. One of the key external relations policy tools available to the European Union is visa liberalization. If Schengen is thrown into doubt, then visa liberalization processes and agreements will also be jeopardized. The existence of Schengen is a strong bargaining tool for the European Union, and its absence would reduce third-country incentives to collaborate with EU

---

48 European Commission, "EU Policy – Background," last updated June 10, 2013, http://ec.europa.eu/enterprise/sectors/tourism/background/.
49 See, for example, the European Data Protection Supervisor, "Opinion on the Proposals for a Regulation establishing an Entry-Exit System (EES) and a Regulation establishing a Registered Traveller Programme (RTP)," Brussels, July 18, 2013, https://secure.edps.europa.eu/EDPSWEB/webdav/site/mySite/shared/Documents/Consultation/Opinions/2013/13-07-18_Smart_borders_EN.pdf.

decrees concerning internal migration management. Given that the European Union has agreed on action plans for visa liberalization with the Ukraine, Russia, Moldova, and potentially Kosovo, this is no small matter.

For all of these reasons, no politician wishes to be at the helm of its demise. While Italy and France were happy to use the politics of brinkmanship once in 2011, it is notable that they were not willing to do so later in the year. In October 2011, when the temporary permits of 22,000 Tunisians were up for renewal, they were quietly extended with little European media coverage.[50]

B. The Difficulty of Dismantling

Schengen would be difficult and costly to dismantle; or rather, internal European borders would be difficult to re-mantle. For countries, particularly in the north, that have become used to allowing traffic through with few checks, the human and financial resources implied by the demise of Schengen would be a huge undertaking.

The Netherlands provides a good example: with a maritime border to the north, land borders with Germany and Belgium, and a major international airport (Schiphol), reinstating border controls, even with the advanced IT infrastructure for registered-traveler systems, would be costly. For instance, the @MigoBoras project to install six mobile and 15 fixed cameras along the motorways linking the Netherlands with Germany and Belgium will cost 19 million euros. In addition, it is not simply a question of reinstalling the system, rehiring border guards, and rebuilding crossing checkpoints; border management infrastructure has transformed since the Netherlands co-created Schengen. For all the Euroskeptic posturing of the Dutch right-wing Party for Freedom (PVV), reintroducing full internal border controls on a permanent and secure basis is not financially viable. And finally, 25 years of cooperation has had an institutional effect on all the actors involved in Schengen, from airport operators to border police. These national organizations are used to cooperating with, and relying upon, one another for information and support.

When discussing issues related to "burden-sharing" and "solidarity," particularly with respect to external border management, it is important that all government actors be reminded of the concrete benefits that Schengen has provided, and the substantial costs that a full collapse would herald. Some calculations in this vein may help to counteract the nationalist politics or concerns over freeloading that have encouraged some policymakers to reassess their commitment to the Schengen area.

---

50 *The Africa News*, "Humanitarian Permits for Tunisians renewed for six months," October 12, 2011, www.theafricanews.com/immigration-news/italy/3312-humanitarian-permits-for-tunisians-renewed-for-six-months.html.

VI. Conclusions and Recommendations

The political high tide of 2011 has subsided, yet the watermarks are still visible. The agreement on the reform of Schengen oversight and function is unlikely to resolve tensions in the long term, and instead papers over the cracks of the current crisis.

There are three interlocking problems at play:

- Schengen cooperation is inextricably linked to the other cooperation systems around Justice and Home Affairs — from information exchange to border management to the Common European Asylum System. A problem in one of these areas becomes a problem for all, and each system will be impossible to complete without the completion of all (on a roughly similar timetable). Fragmented negotiations on individual proposals hinder Member States from seeing the interlocking systems in their entirety. However, if seen as a whole, the enormity of the project is daunting.

- Member States have committed to cooperating in the area of border management, one of the most sensitive areas of national sovereignty. However, they have done so with the caveat that their individual autonomy to act and make executive decisions must not be disturbed. This fundamental incompatibility has to be resolved or managed before common systems can develop further, and Member States should recognize that the institutional machinery that has grown up around national administrations, from the European Court of Human Rights to Frontex, is likely to make it less easy to pursue independent action in the future.

- Member States desire robust rules and mechanisms to keep other states in line, yet refuse to cede power to an independent institution to manage the monitoring and evaluation of Schengen impartially, transparently, and objectively. To avoid the inevitable politics of collaboration, Member States should step back from the front line of Schengen supervision. For its part, the European Commission has yet to demonstrate that its supervision of Schengen would be effective and workable.

Before considering the next phase of the Schengen system, Member States must independently weigh the value of this public good against current levels of national autonomy and interest. For Schengen to continue in its present form there needs to be recognition that reintroducing internal borders on a permanent basis is a luxury that few (if any) European countries can afford, but that adjustment to a more efficient, unified system promises to be politically unpleasant. Any major improvement, however, will require a significant philosophical and political shift in approach from all parties.

In the absence of a visible commitment and common consensus on addressing Europe's immigration flows, continued Schengen cooperation (as it is currently experienced) will be harder and harder to maintain, particularly as Member States are likely to continue to refer to domestic politics when negotiating at the EU level. Of course, a "Schengen lite" may be pursued, whereby regional blocs continue to collaborate without borders, or information-exchange mechanisms continue alongside a modified increase in borders and customs checks. Indeed, it may be that saving Schengen comes at a price too high for Member States, who do not always incorporate the value of public goods in their cost-benefit analyses.

In order to achieve stability within the Schengen system, Member States will have to further relinquish autonomy to an independent EU actor. Excepting immediate crises of public security, an objective agent is needed to determine the legitimacy of internal border controls. The type of actor, and the mechanism through which greater equity and oversight might be achieved, is an open question. As a straightforward delegation of the European Commission has already proved to be unacceptable, other options need to be found; indeed, some experts have floated a number of possible designs to minimize "gaming" the system.[51]

But checks and balances are not enough. Good behavior is also necessary. Continued Schengen cooperation is predicated on three separate factors: trust, equity, and low political salience, all of which are at a premium in the current EU political climate. Inflammatory public statements and short-term political games don't just damage the Schengen system but also harm relationships among Member States and jeopardize future collaboration in related policy fields.

The current debates surrounding Schengen insinuate that the costs of securing the benefits of internal free movement and security have become too high. Rather, it seems that Member States have undervalued the good that Schengen presents to them as individual countries, and as a core symbol of European integration. Once the direct and indirect benefits of the free movement of people and goods across borders — and the costs of reinstating internal border controls — have been accounted for, Member States benefit more than they perhaps realize. In this context, closer collaboration is not only necessary for Schengen to survive, but desirable for the good of all.

---

51 See, for example, Haake, Kreiger, and Minter, "External Border Enforcement, Public Goods and Burden Sharing Mechanisms in the EU."

Works Cited

BBC News. 2006. France Urges EU Immigration Curbs. September 29, 2006. http://news.bbc.co.uk/2/hi/europe/5391920.stm.

Blair, Tony. 2003. Letter from United Kingdom Prime Minister Tony Blair to Greek Prime Minister Costas Simitis. March 10, 2003. www.statewatch.org/news/2003/apr/blair-simitis-asile.pdf.

Collignon, Stefan. 2011. The Governance of European Public Goods. In *The EU Budget: What Should Go In? What Should Go Out?* ed. Daniel Tarschys. Stockholm: Swedish Institute for European Policy Studies. www.sieps.se/sites/default/files/2011_3.pdf.

Council of Europe, Parliamentary Assembly Committee on Migration, Refugees and Population. 2007. Assessment of Transit and Processing Centres as a Response to Mixed Flows of Migrants and Asylum Seekers. June 13, 2007. http://assembly.coe.int/ASP/Doc/XrefViewHTML.asp?FileID=11557&Language=EN.

Council of the European Union. 2012. Amended Proposal for a Regulation of the European Parliament and of the Council on the Establishment of an Evaluation and Monitoring Mechanism to Verify the Application of the Schengen Acquis. Brussels, June 4, 2012. http://register.consilium.europa.eu/pdf/en/12/st05/st05754-re06.en12.pdf.

_____. 2012. Common responses to current challenges by Member States most affected by secondary mixed migration flows. Brussels, March 9, 2012. Accessed from Statewatch, www.statewatch.org/news/2012/mar/eu-council-secondary-migration-flows-7431-12.pdf.

Dutch Ministry of the Interior. 2012. Factsheet Gebruik @migoboras. The Hague, February 9, 2012. www.rijksoverheid.nl/bestanden/documenten-en-publicaties/brochures/2012/02/09/factsheet-gebruik-migoboras/20120127-factsheet-migo-boras.pdf.

European Commission. 2006. Council Decision of 5 October 2006 on the Establishment of a Mutual Information Mechanism Concerning Member States' Measures in the Areas of Asylum and Immigration. October 5, 2006, EUR-Lex, http://eur-lex.europa.eu/LexUriServ/LexUriServ.do?uri=CELEX:32006D0688:EN:NOT.

_____. 2010. *Study on the Feasibility of Establishing a Mechanism for Relocation of the Beneficiaries of International Protection*. Copenhagen: Ramboll Management Consulting and Eurasylum Limited. http://ec.europa.eu/home-affairs/doc_centre/asylum/docs/final_report_relocation_of_refugees.pdf.

_____. 2011. Communication on Migration. Brussels, May 4, 2011. http://ec.europa.eu/home-affairs/news/intro/docs/1_EN_ACT_part1_v11.pdf.

_____. 2011. Proposal for a Regulation of the European Parliament and of the Council Amending Regulation (EC) No. 562/2006 in Order to Provide for Common Rules on the Temporary Reintroduction of Border Control at Internal Borders in Exceptional Circumstances. Brussels, December 9, 2011. http://ec.europa.eu/dgs/home-affairs/e-library/docs/pdf/560_en_en.pdf.

_____. 2011. Schengen Governance — Strengthening the Area without Internal Border Control. Brussels, September 16, 2011. EUR-Lex, http://eur-lex.europa.eu/LexUriServ/LexUriServ.do?uri=COM:2011:0561:FIN:EN:PDF.

_____. 2011. The European Commission's Response to the Migratory Flows from North Africa. News release, April 8, 2011. http://europa.eu/rapid/press-release_MEMO-11-226_en.htm.

_____. 2013. EU Policy – Background, http://ec.europa.eu/enterprise/sectors/tourism/background/. Last updated June 10, 2013.

European Council. 2011. Council Conclusions: 23/24 June 2011. EUCO 23/11. Brussels, June 24, 2011. http://ec.europa.eu/commission_2010-2014/president/news/speeches-statements/pdf/20110624_1_en.pdf.

_____. 2013. Council and the European Parliament reach a provisional agreement on the Schengen Governance legislative package. Brussels, May 30, 2013. www.consilium.europa.eu/uedocs/cms_data/docs/pressdata/en/jha/137348.pdf.

European Council on Refugees and Exiles. 2010. Asylum lottery in the EU in 2010. http://ecre.org/component/content/article/56-ecre-actions/246-asylum-lottery-in-the-eu-in-2010.html.

European Court of Human Rights. 2011. *Case of M.S.S. vs. Belgium and Greece:* Judgment. Strasbourg, January 21, 2011. http://hudoc.echr.coe.int/sites/eng/pages/search.aspx?i=001-103050.

European Parliament, Committee on Civil Liberties, Justice and Home Affairs. 2011. Draft Report on the Proposal for a Regulation of the European Parliament and of the Council on the Establishment of an Evaluation Mechanism to Verify Application of the Schengen Acquis. Brussels, April 13, 2011. www.europarl.europa.eu/meetdocs/2009_2014/documents/libe/pr/860/860326/860326en.pdf.

European Parliament, Policy Department C: Citizens' Rights and Constitutional Affairs. 2011. *Implementation of the EU Charter of Fundamental Rights and its Impact on EU Home Affairs Agencies: Frontex, Europol and the European Asylum Support Office.* Brussels: European Parliament. www.ceps.eu/ceps/dld/6312/pdf.

European Parliament. 2011. Schengen: stricter EU rules to prevent illegal border checks. November 29, 2011, www.europarl.europa.eu/news/en/pressroom/content/20111129IPR32707/html/Schengen-stricter-EU-rules-to-prevent-illegal-border-checks.

European Parliament. 2012. EP suspends cooperation with Council following decision on Schengen area rules. June 13, 2012. www.europarl.europa.eu/news/en/headlines/content/20120613STO46764/html/EP-suspends-cooperation-with-Council-following-decision-on-Schengen-area-rules.

Fargues, Philippe and Christine Fandrich. 2012. *Migration after the Arab Spring.* MPC Research Report 2012/09. www.migrationpolicycentre.eu/docs/MPC 2012 EN 09.pdf.

Foulkes, Christopher D. 2012. Australia's Boat People: Asylum Challenges and Two Decades of Policy Experimentation. *Migration Information Source,* July 2012. http://migrationinformation.org/Feature/display.cfm?ID=899.

Frontex. 2010. Frontex to Deploy 175 Specialist Border Personnel to Greece. October 29, 2010. www.frontex.europa.eu/news/frontex-to-deploy-175-specialist-border-personnel-to-greece-9neidF.

_____. 2011. *RABIT Operation 2010 Evaluation Report*. Warsaw: Frontex. www.frontex.europa.eu/assets/Attachments_News/fer_rabit_2010_screen_v6.pdf.

_____. Undated. Archive of Joint Operations. www.frontex.europa.eu/operations/types-of-operations/general.

Haake, Claus-Jochen, Tim Krieger, and Steffen Minter. 2010. External Border Enforcement, Public Goods and Burden Sharing Mechanisms in the EU. In *Shaping the Normative Contours of the European Union: A Migration-Border Framework*, ed. Richard Zapato-Barrera. Barcelona: Barcelona Centre for International Affairs. www.cidob.org/en/publications/monographs/monographs/shaping_the_normative_contours_of_the_european_union_a_migration_border_framework.

Human Rights Watch. 2011. *The EU's Dirty Hands: Frontex Involvement in Ill-Treatment of Migrant Detainees in Greece*. Brussels: Human Rights Watch. www.hrw.org/node/101671/section/1.

Lutterbeck, Derek. 2009. Small Frontier Island: Malta and the Challenge of Irregular Immigration. *Mediterranean Quarterly* 20 (1): 119–44.

Molodikova, Irina. 2008. Patterns of East to West Migration in the Context of European Migration Systems: Possibilities and Limits of Migration Control. *Demográfia* 51 (5) English Edition: 5–35.

Nielsen, Nikolaj. 2012. Sarkozy Threatens to End EU Passport-Free Travel. *Euobserver*, March 12, 2012. http://euobserver.com/9/115556.

Papademetriou, Demetrios G. and Elizabeth Collett. 2011. *A New Architecture for Border Management*. Washington, DC: Migration Policy Institute. www.migrationpolicy.org/pubs/borderarchitecture.pdf.

Parkin, Joanna. 2011. *The Difficult Road to the Schengen Information System II: The Legacy of "Laboratories" and the Cost for Fundamental Rights and the Rule of Law*. Brussels: Centre for European Policy Studies. www.ceps.eu/ceps/dld/4373/pdf.

Rettman, Andrew. 2013. Criminals Exploiting EU Travel Freedoms, Dutch Data Shows. *EUobserver*, March 15, 2013. http://euobserver.com/justice/119440.

Sarkozy, Nicolas and Silvio Berlusconi. 2011. Joint letter from Nicolas Sarkozy, President of the Republic, and Silvio Berlusconi, Prime Minister of Italy, to Herman Van Rompuy, President of the European Council, and José Manuel Barroso, President of the European Commission. Rome, April 26, 2011. www.ambafrance-uk.org/Letter-from-French-and-Italian.

Sushko, Iryna, Olexiy Vradiy, Oleksandr Sushko, Volodymyr Kipen, Svitlana Mitryayeva, Andriy Lepak, and Andriy Matyukhanov. 2010. *Schengen Consulates in Assessments and Ratings. Visa Practices of the EU Member States in Ukraine*. Kiev: Europe without Barriers. http://novisa.com.ua/upload/file/Viza_Monitor_ENG-3.pdf.

The Africa News. 2011. Humanitarian Permits for Tunisians renewed for six months. October 12, 2011. www.theafricanews.com/immigration-news/italy/3312-humanitarian-permits-for-tunisians-renewed-for-six-months.html.

Thielemann, Eiko and Carolyn Armstrong. 2013. Understanding European Asylum Cooperation under the Schengen/Dublin System: A Public Goods Framework. *European Security* 22 (2): 148-64.

Treaty of Amsterdam Amending the Treaty of the European Union, the Treaties Establishing the European Communities and Certain Related Acts. November 10, 1997, EUR-Lex 340/1. http://eur-lex.europa.eu/en/treaties/dat/11997D/tif/JOC_1997_340__1_EN_0005.pdf.

United Nations High Commissioner for Refugees (UNHCR). 2011. *Asylum Levels and Trends in Industrialized Countries*. Geneva: UNHCR. www.unhcr.org/4fdf1b779.html.

_____. 2013. Number of Syrian Refugees tops 2 million mark with more on the way. Press Release, September 13, 2013. www.unhcr.org/522495669.html.

ACKNOWLEDGMENTS

The editors would like to thank the policymakers and immigration and border security experts who participated in the two-day workshop on "Security and Borders: Policy and Politics" which took place in Berlin on March 22-23, 2012. The workshop was hosted at the Embassy of Canada to Germany and jointly sponsored by the Migration Policy Institute (MPI) and the Canada Centre for Global Security Studies at the University of Toronto's Munk School of Global Affairs.

The chapters in this volume were written to inform this workshop, which explored the security challenges raised by porous borders, how states are responding to these challenges, and the complexities of reducing security threats while maintaining the efficient movement of people and goods. The ideas and recommendations within the chapters are the authors' own and do not necessarily represent the views of MPI or the Munk School of Global Affairs.

The editors would like to thank the authors for their thoughtful and insightful contributions to this work. They also thank Kate Brick, who nurtured this project before and after the workshop in Berlin; and Natalia Banulescu-Bogdan and Sarah Flamm for helping coordinate the book project and seeing it to completion.

About the Editors

Randall Hansen is Director of the Centre for European, Russian, and Eurasian Studies, Munk School of Global Affairs, and Full Research Professor and Canada Research Chair in Immigration and Governance in the Department of Political Science at the University of Toronto. His research examines migration, population policy, and the effect of war on civilian populations. His recent published works include *Sterilized by the State: Eugenics, Race and the Population Scare in 20th Century North America* (Cambridge University Press, 2014); *Disobeying Hitler: German Resistance after July 20, 1944* (Oxford University Press, 2013); *Fire and Fury: The Allied Bombing of Germany* (Penguin, 2009); and *Citizenship and Immigration in Post-War Britain* (Oxford University Press, 2000).

He has co-edited *Immigration and Public Opinion in Liberal Democracies* (with David Leal and Gary P. Freeman, Routledge, 2012); *Migration, States and International Cooperation* (with Jeannette Money and Jobst Koehler, Routledge, 2011); *Immigration and Asylum from 1900 to the Present* (with Matthew Gibney; ABC-CLIO, 2005); *Dual Nationality, Social Rights, and Federal Citizenship in the U.S. and Europe* (with Patrick Weil, Berghahn, 2002); and *Towards a European Nationality* (with Patrick Weil, Palgrave, 2001).

Dr. Hansen is also the author of several articles on immigration, citizenship, and asylum published in *World Politics, Comparative Political Studies*, and the *European Journal of Political Research*. He previously taught at the Universities of London (Queen Mary), Oxford (where he was a tutorial fellow at Merton College), and Newcastle (where he held an established Chair).

Demetrios G. Papademetriou is President and Co-Founder of the Migration Policy Institute (MPI). He is also President of Migration Policy Institute Europe — a nonprofit, independent research institute in Brussels that aims to promote a better understanding of migration trends and effects within Europe — and serves on MPI Europe's Administrative Council. Dr. Papademetriou is the convener of the Transatlantic Council on Migration, which is composed of senior public figures, business leaders, and public intellectuals from Europe, the United States, and Canada. He also convenes and codirects the Regional Migration Study Group, a joint initiative of MPI and the Woodrow Wilson Center that in 2013 proposed new regional and collaborative approaches to migration, competitiveness, and human-capital development for the United States, Central America, and Mexico.

Dr. Papademetriou is Co-Founder and International Chair Emeritus of *Metropolis: An International Forum for Research and Policy on Migration and Cities*, and has served as Chair of the World Economic Forum's Global Agenda Council on Migration (2009-11); Chair of the Migration Committee of the Organization for Economic Cooperation and Development (OECD); Director for Immigration Policy and Research at the US Department of Labor and Chair of the Secretary of Labor's Immigration Policy Task Force; and Executive Editor of the *International Migration Review*.

Dr. Papademetriou has published more than 250 books, articles, monographs, and research reports on migration topics and advises senior government and political party officials in more than 20 countries (including numerous European Union Member States while they hold the rotating EU presidency).

He holds a PhD in comparative public policy and international relations, and has taught at the universities of Maryland, Duke, American, and in the New School for Social Research.

About the Authors

Elizabeth Collett is Director of Migration Policy Institute Europe, headquartered in Brussels, and is also Senior Advisor to MPI's Transatlantic Council on Migration. Based in Brussels, Ms. Collett focuses on European migration and immigrant integration policy.

Prior to joining MPI, Ms. Collett was a Senior Policy Analyst at the European Policy Centre, an independent Brussels-based think tank, and was responsible for its migration program, which covered all aspects of European migration and integration policy. During her time at EPC she produced numerous working papers and policy briefs focused on the future of European Union immigration policy. She has also worked in the Migration Research and Policy Department of the International Organization (IOM) for Migration in Geneva and for the Institute for the Study of International Migration in Washington, DC.

Ms. Collett, who is a Research Associate at Compas, Oxford University, holds a master's degree in foreign service (with distinction) from Georgetown University, where she specialized in foreign policy and earned a certificate in refugee and humanitarian studies, and a bachelor's degree in law from Oxford University.

Ralph Espach is a senior research scientist and Director of the Latin American Affairs program at the Center for Strategic Studies at the Center for Naval Analyses (CNA). CNA is a federally funded research and development center (FFRDC) for the US Navy and Marine Corps in Alexandria, VA.

Dr. Espach's recent research includes criminal organizations in Central America, motivations of FARC (Revolutionary Armed Forces of Colombia) members for joining and leaving the insurgency in Colombia, the implications of China's growing presence in Latin America for US and regional security, and the security implications of climate change for

Latin American countries. He contributes frequently to media on Latin American security issues, both in the United States and in the region. He is the author of *Private Environmental Regimes in Developing Countries: Globally Sown, Locally Grown* (Palgrave-Macmillan, 2009) and co-editor of *The Strategic Dynamics of Latin American Trade* (Stanford University Press, 2004); *Latin America in the New International System* (Lynne Rienner Publishers, 2000); and *Combating Corruption in Latin America* (Johns Hopkins University Press, 2000).

Dr. Espach holds a PhD in political science from the University of California, Berkeley and a BA from Columbia College in New York City.

Brian Grant is former Deputy Director of the International Program at the Migration Policy Institute in Washington, D.C. Prior to joining MPI, he was the Director General of International and Intergovernmental Relations at Citizenship and Immigration Canada (CIC). In this capacity, he was responsible for Canada's engagement on international migration issues as well as for CIC's relations with provincial and territorial governments, which share jurisdiction over immigration under the Canadian Constitution. Before assuming this post in September 2007, Mr. Grant was the Director General of Strategic Policy and Partnerships at CIC. He also worked for the United Kingdom Immigration Service in London from 1999 to 2001, and over the previous decade held a number of positions within the enforcement area of CIC. He was the lead negotiator for Canada on the migration chapter of the North American Free Trade Agreement.

Mr. Grant began his public service career in 1984 as an information officer with Employment and Immigration Canada, and holds a bachelor's degree from Carleton University and a master's from the University of Leeds.

Daniel Haering is Director of the Ibn Khaldún International Research Center at the Francisco Marroquín University in Guatemala City, Guatemala. He also is a professor at the Institute of Political Studies and International Relations, where he teaches New Concepts of Security and Methodology. His research focuses on Guatemala's political system and the impact of organized crime in rural areas, with special attention on drug-trafficking organizations in Central America.

Kay Hailbronner was Chair of Public Law, Public International Law, and European Law at the University of Konstanz and Director of the Centre for International and European Law on Immigration and Asylum. He is also a holder of a Jean-Monnet Chair of European Law and a Robert Schumann Chair on EU-China relations. His research focuses on national and international migrants and asylum law, citizenship, university legislation, regulation for awarding contracts as well as on European law. He is co-editor of the leading journal on migrant law in Germany.

Christopher Sands is a Senior Fellow at the Hudson Institute in Washington, D.C., where he specializes on Canada and US-Canadian relations, and directs the Hudson Institute's Initiative on North American Competitiveness. He is also a professorial lecturer at the Johns Hopkins University School of Advanced International Studies, an adjunct professor in government at the American University School of Public Affairs, and lecturer at the Foreign Service Institute of the US Department of State and the US Department of Homeland Security. For the 2012-13 academic year, Dr. Sands was the G. Robert Ross Distinguished Visiting Professor of Canada-US Business and Economics in the College of Business and Economics at Western Washington University in Bellingham, WA.

From 2002 to 2007, he was the Director of Strategic Planning and Evaluation at the International Republican Institute (IRI), a core institute of the National Endowment for Democracy and implementer of democracy and governance programs of the US Agency for International Development (USAID) and Department of State.

Dr. Sands holds a BA in political science from Macalester College in St. Paul, MN, and an MA and PhD in Canadian studies and international economics from the Paul H. Nitze School of Advanced International Studies at the Johns Hopkins University.

Louise Shelley is a Professor in the School of Public Policy at George Mason University. She directs the Terrorism, Transnational Crime and Corruption Center (TraCCC), which she founded in 1998. Her research focuses on corruption, human trafficking, illicit trade, terrorism, transnational crime, and the former Soviet Union.

Since 1995, Dr. Shelley has run programs with leading specialists on the problems of organized crime and corruption in Russia, the Ukraine, and Georgia. She has also been the principal investigator of large-scale projects on money laundering from Russia, the Ukraine, and Georgia and of training law enforcement in human trafficking.

She is the author of *Human Trafficking: A Global Perspective* (Cambridge, 2010), *Policing Soviet Society* (Routledge, 1996), *Lawyers in Soviet Work Life* (Rutgers University Press, 1984), and *Crime and Modernization* (Southern Illinois University Press, 1981), as well as numerous articles and book chapters on various aspects of transnational crime and corruption. Dr. Shelley is a member of the Council on Foreign Relations and serves on the boards of *Demokratizatsiya: The Journal of Post-Soviet Democratization*, the *European Journal on Criminal Policy and Research*, *Global Crime,* and the *International Annals of Criminology*.

About the Migration Policy Institute

The Migration Policy Institute is an independent, nonpartisan, nonprofit think tank in Washington, DC dedicated to analysis of the movement of people worldwide.

MPI provides analysis, development, and evaluation of migration and refugee policies at the local, national, and international levels. It aims to meet the rising demand for pragmatic and thoughtful responses to the challenges and opportunities that large-scale migration, whether voluntary or forced, presents to communities and institutions in an increasingly integrated world.

Founded in 2001 by Demetrios G. Papademetriou and Kathleen Newland, MPI grew out of the International Migration Policy Program at the Carnegie Endowment for International Peace.

MPI is guided by the philosophy that international migration needs active and intelligent management. When such policies are in place and are responsibly administered, they bring benefits to immigrants and their families, communities of origin and destination, and sending and receiving countries.

MPI's policy research and analysis proceed from four central propositions:

- Fair, smart, transparent, and rights-based immigration and refugee policies can promote social cohesion, economic vitality, and national security.

- Given the opportunity, immigrants become net contributors and create new social and economic assets.

- Sound immigration and integration policies result from balanced analysis, solid data, and the engagement of a spectrum of stakeholders — from community leaders and immigrant organizations to the policy elite — interested in immigration policy and its human consequences.

- National policymaking benefits from international comparative research, as more and more countries accumulate data, analysis, and policy experience related to global migration.

MPI's International Program acts as a policy laboratory for developing innovative, evidence-based, and politically feasible solutions to worldwide migration policy challenges. From advising countries holding the rotating EU Presidency on migration and immigrant integration matters to crafting policy memos for national governments rethinking their border or citizenship policies, MPI's International Program strives to inform ongoing policy debates in North and Central America, Europe, and Asia, as well as at the global level.

For more on MPI's mission, experts, and research, visit: www.migrationpolicy.org.

About the Munk School of Global Affairs, University of Toronto

The Munk School of Global Affairs is a professional degree-granting interdisciplinary school focused on global issues. The Munk School's mission is to deeply integrate research on global affairs with teaching and public education.

The Munk School is home to world-renowned researchers and academic centers, including the Asian Institute; the Canada Centre for Global Security Studies; the India Innovation Institute; the Citizen Lab; the Centre for European, Russian, and Eurasian Studies; and over 40 other centers, institutes, and programs.

The centerpiece of the Munk School's academic core is the highly selective master of global affairs (MGA) program. The MGA invites the very best of Canada and the world's students to complete a groundbreaking two-year program that incorporates campus-based study with mandatory global internships in their chosen field.

For more about the Munk School, please visit: www.munkschool.utoronto.ca/.